Praise for

MOVE THE
NEEDLE

"This is an adventure story of yarn, entrepreneurship, hustle, and family . . . *Move the Needle* overflows with passion, wisdom, and hard-won business (and life) lessons."

— **Jeff Walker**, #1 *New York Times* best-selling author of *Launch*

"If only this book had existed when I started my business! Shelley's story is not only inspiring, but has a way of making the reader feel less alone in their own challenges"

— **Laura Zander**, co-founder and CEO, Jimmy Beans Wool

"If you've ever felt like you were meant to do more, but you just weren't sure what your next step should be, let me tell you . . . it's reading this book! This book is about *you* taking a chance on yourself. Even when everyone around you says you 'can't' do something, Shelley demonstrates that with a little creativity and courage, the impossible becomes possible."

— **Stu McLaren**, membership expert and creator of TRIBE

"*Move The Needle* is a call to action that inspires, entertains, and encourages. This story challenged me to take that first step. Well done, Shelley."

— **Gaye Glasspie**, founder and CEO, GGMadeIt

"Shelley is like your best friend who sits you down, pours you a glass of wine, spills her juiciest secrets, then gives you exactly the kick in the pants you need to put your wildest dreams into motion"

— **Amy Porterfield**, entrepreneur and podcast host of
Online Marketing Made Easy

"Once I started reading, I couldn't stop! From the very first yarn, where four-year-old Shelley makes her way to the grocery store on her tricycle after being told she can't go, we are given a window into a brilliant, empathic, and creative mind, heart and soul that always finds a way. If you are looking for inspiration to trust yourself more, take brave action, tap into your passion like never before, and make your own path, this is *exactly* the book you need to read right now. It's real. It's powerful. It's a joyful experience. I love this book!"

— **Michelle Falzon**, founder of We Are Content and creator of Create Without Burnout

"Shelley shares with us her creative and entrepreneurial journey in a way that makes us identify with her every step of the way. Her stories, experiences, and advice are strong, and she offers an empowering message, especially for those of us who are trying to make our way through life freelancing and building our own projects. This book will move you and help you find the determination to make that dream of yours come true."

— **Joji Locatelli**, knitwear designer

"One of many gifts I got from *Move the Needle* is a message I needed to hear: that character is something we build from our experiences, and if we keep working at it, good things come. The tiny girl who took off on her tricycle to the store kept trying, and she got to a lot of interesting places."

— **Kay Gardiner**, co-founder, Modern Daily Knitting

"I once believed that 'creatives' couldn't make real money . . . this book proves otherwise! A brilliant combination of anecdotal stories, firsthand experience, and heartwarming lessons all wonderfully woven together."

— **Shaa Wasmund**, best-selling author of *Stop Talking, Start Doing*

"A brilliant collection of stories and lessons that demonstrate how to achieve your dreams in business, live a more fulfilling life, and how to be a better, kinder person."

— **Dylan Frost**, creator of the Wholesale Formula

"A must-read for any creative person who wants to make a significant income from their passion and craft. After reading this book, you will see how in this new world, creatives have the unfair advantage! Shelley reveals how this counterintuitive way of achieving success is no longer a result of hard work and traditional skills. Embrace your creative skills and enjoy the rewards in whatever way fills your heart."

— **Michael Maidens**, best-selling author, co-creator of
The Abundance Code film, and creator of Offer Academy

"Shelley takes us on a thoroughly entertaining journey full of life lessons and inspiration to show us that passion, persistence, and creativity can lead to *any* of us achieving our dreams. I love this book and definitely recommend it."

— **Kat Coroy**, founder and CEO, Instagram Makeover

"Shelley's story is the perfect prescription for how people need to look at their lives, understanding that we all only get one and that following your instinct and passion is always the best prescription for success. Don't mistake this book as being a small story about a small niche. *Move the Needle* is a yarn of epic proportions, told by an epic entrepreneur, with heart and love."

— **Brian Kurtz**, founder, Titans Marketing, author of *Overdeliver* and co-author of *The Advertising Solution*

"From the outside looking in, I would never have thought that Shelley ever had these kinds of struggles. Her story was refreshing, comforting, and also incredibly inspiring—like she got through all of this, and so can I! What I'm still left thinking about is the way she thought so big and held to her unique, creative vision and just didn't take no for an answer. Calling us to get more mentors and to delegate what is not our strong suit felt like a direct message from Shelley to me."

— **Amy Small**, founder and CEO, Knit Collage

"What this book is really about is: tenacity, enthusiasm, and passionately believing in your own 'crazy' creative visions. Shelley encourages you to just start with your big, bold vision front and center, and her story powerfully illustrates how you too can make success appear in your life stitch by stitch, row by row. This is a must-read for all entrepreneurs, visionaries, and creatives. I remained riveted until the very end."

— **Julie Ann Cairns**, best-selling author of *The Abundance Code* and director of *The Abundance Code* documentary series

"*Wow!* As someone who always heard the word can't and pushed harder; as someone who has instinctively never stopped, even when (and especially when) told no; and as someone who cherishes creativity, empathy, and integrity, I learned so much more about myself and my journey from Shelley's story. This book is a must-read for anyone who has a dream of making things better, of making the world a better place, and for anyone who just loves to reach for something big!"

— **Jason Friedman**, founder and CEO, CXFormula, LLC

"Shelley Brander is like a buttercup of creative goodness combined with a laser beam of business shrewdness."

— **Victoria Labalme**, author and creator of Risk Forward® and Rock The Room®

"This is the book our world needs right now—it's going to be the catalyst for so many new, passion-driven businesses. If Shelley can do this with yarn, you can do this with your own passion no matter how improbable it may seem."

— **Susan Peirce Thompson**, Ph.D. founder and CEO, Bright Line Eating

"This is an awesome story and would make a great reality show! I cannot believe how much drama exists in the knitting world. But it's also a great way to get to know Shelley. Like a Netflix binge-watch, I had to read it in one sitting— I could not wait to see what happened."

— **Rich McFarland**, CEO, Rich Embrace Media

"It is Shelley's cheerful determination, impressive warmth, and good humor, all coupled with drive and enviable marketing skills, that has carried her from being a newbie yarn shop owner and mother to creating Knit Stars and a global family of knitters. This book is quite a journey: kick back and enjoy the adventure."

— **Lucy Neatby**, knitting guru

"I love this book! I could not put it down. I knew this was going to be a great read when the intro ended with 'hang on to your handlebars and let's go for a ride.' If you're a creative who's been told, 'You can't,' then following Shelley's journey is a ride you need to take. She shows us all the ways we 'can' in a collection of stories that both entertain and inspire. If you've cherished your first venture into making in all its imperfections, you'll relish hearing about the Orangutan Sweater and its extra-long sleeves. But the most important message you'll take away is that your creativity matters. That by embracing our own unique value and being brave enough to share it with the world, we can save the world."

— **Mary Gilkerson**, painter, teacher, entrepreneur

"The unique mix of endearing, personal stories, and em-bedded life lessons on creativity and courage will not only draw you in but leave you feeling inspired to take bold action to *Move the Needle* in your own life."

— **Ryan Levesque**, three-time Inc. 5000 CEO and #1 national best-selling author of *Ask* and *Choose*

"The title says it all. If you are ready to move the needle in your own life and to be inspired, then you have found the right book. Shelly is the real deal, and I am so thankful she wrote this book."

— **Mark Timm**, serial entrepreneur and co-author of *Mentor to Millions*

MOVE THE NEEDLE

Also by Shelley Brander

Untangled: A Step-by-Step Guide to Joy and Success for the Modern Yarn Lover

MOVE THE NEEDLE

Yarns from an Unlikely Entrepreneur

SHELLEY BRANDER

HAY HOUSE, INC.
Carlsbad, California • New York City
London • Sydney • New Delhi

Copyright © 2021 by Shelley Brander

Published in the United States by: Hay House, Inc.: www.hayhouse.com®
Published in Australia by: Hay House Australia Pty. Ltd.: www.hay house
.com.au • **Published in the United Kingdom by:** Hay House UK, Ltd.:
www.hayhouse.co.uk • **Published in India by:** Hay House Publishers
India: www.hayhouse.co.in

Project editor: Melody Guy • *Indexer:* Laura Ogar
Cover design: The Book Designers • *Interior design:* Nick C. Welch
Interior photos/illustrations: All photos printed are courtesy of the author.

Cataloging-in-Publication Data is on file at the Library of Congress

Hardcover ISBN: 978-1-4019-6055-1
E-book ISBN: 978-1-4019-6054-4
Audiobook ISBN: 978-1-4019-6076-6

10 9 8 7 6 5 4 3 2 1
1st edition, January 2021

Printed in the United States of America

To Mallory, Cec, and Sam.
You move me.
Every day.

CONTENTS

Your Third Move: When Things Unravel

Your Fourth Move: Nurturing the Creative Team

INTRODUCTION

One of my earliest memories is from when I was about four years old. I remember being really, really bored, and then I heard my mom's keys jangle. So I ran to find her in the kitchen and asked where she was going.

"Just running to the grocery for a couple of things," she said.

"Oh pleeeeeeeease, can I come too?" I begged.

"It's just a really quick trip. Sorry, you can't come this time."

Can't. Even so long ago, even at such a tender young age, I remember this word triggering something really powerful inside of me. Something primal. Something fierce. But instead of throwing a tantrum, or retreating to my room and crying, I made a plan.

I WAS going to that grocery store.

My dad was sitting with his feet propped up in the orange-and-gold striped recliner, circa 1972, reading the newspaper. I told him I was going out to get the mail. (Our mailbox was out by the curb, so I knew this would buy me a little time.) He peeked over his paper and nodded, oblivious to my scheming.

Then I marched my four-year-old self to our garage, straddled my trusty tricycle, and pedaled to the mailbox. (See, Daddy? I went to the mailbox just as I'd promised.) I retrieved the mail (there was more than I expected—must have been junk mail day), tucked it into my shirt, and continued to pedal down the street.

I took a turn, and then another. And then I took a deep breath.

It was time to cross 51st Street.

At the time, this was one of the busiest streets in Tulsa, Oklahoma (still is). Cars whipped by in all directions. I waited . . . waited . . . waited . . . the letters and magazines were poking me uncomfortably under my T-shirt.

Then I saw my chance. In my mind, I took off like a rocket. But on my tricycle, with my stubby four-year-old legs, it probably looked more like a turtle trying to escape a predator. It was fast by turtle standards—just not quite fast enough. Cars were braking and honking . . . but I made it across. Then I turned to continue pedaling toward the grocery, against traffic. Just a couple more blocks to go . . . .

Me on my trusty tricyle, circa 1972.

And then one of the oncoming cars pulled over right in front of me.

Uh-oh, it was Mom.

The jig was up.

To this day, my mom finds a way to tell this story every time she introduces me to one of her friends. "I saw this little girl on her tricycle, and my first thought was, what kind of mother would let her child do this?

"My next thought was, that looks like Shelley.

"And then, OH MY GOD, that is Shelley!"

When we got back home, I brought the mail to my dad. And then *he* brought a switch he'd pulled straight off a pecan tree in our yard, right down on my bare behind.

Did that pecan branch teach me a lesson? Well, maybe— but not the one my father intended. I look back at that little girl on the tricycle and I realize, something solidified that day. Deep inside, something took shape: the awareness that I wasn't inextricably tied to my home, my family, *the rules*. I could break free. Make my own way.

My life has taken some pretty crazy twists and turns. From hyper, awkward child to insecure cheerleader and sorority girl. From newspaper morgue intern to warehouse schlepper to ice cream scooper. From terrified wife and young mom of an autistic baby to passionate mom to three spectacularly creative, kind, and beautiful young adults. From writing local car commercials to building global brands for others, to building an ultra-positive, international maker community aligned with my own crazy passion for knitting.

The story, whenever I'm telling it and now that I'm writing it, can seem pretty unbelievable. I pinch myself. Every. Single. Day. And it all began with a single word:

Can't.

As I mapped out this book, over and over again, I saw the word popping up:

You *can't* go to the store with me.

You *can't* be a creative director as a woman.

You *can't* cure autism.

You *can't* make a living in yarn.

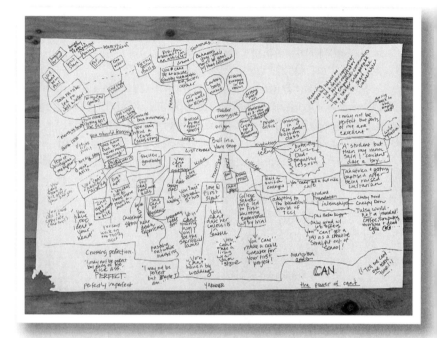

My initial mind map for *Move the Needle*.

"Can't" was the gasoline that poured on my life, that time and time again, ignited me. That fueled me through the darkest times and drove me to keep following my gut. Beat the odds. Prove them all wrong.

For a long time, I was afraid to admit this. To be driven by the "can'ts" of others sounded negative, combative, competitive, emotional. All the things I grew up being told *not* to be. But looking back now, it's undeniable.

As Steve Jobs famously said, "You can't connect the dots looking forward; you can only connect them looking backward." And now it's clear that many of my life's most critical moments were the ones that seemed crazy and weird and even defiant to everyone else around me at the time.

In these moments, I trusted my truest self. My bravest self. My most creative self. I said to hell with the rules, ignored convention, listened to my heart, and lit my own path.

In this book, I'll share the stories that shaped me as a person, a wife and mother, a creative, and ultimately, as an entrepreneur leading Loops and Knit Stars, two global craft businesses, and a movement to Knit the World Together. I'll be nakedly transparent about both the wins and the failures. And I'll share the lessons I didn't even realize that life was teaching me at the time.

My hope is that this book will inspire you to trust your own creativity, flow with the seemingly random twists and turns that life throws at you, and discover and fully live your own passion and purpose.

So hang on to your handlebars, and let's go for a ride.

Your First Move

BELIEVING
IN YOUR
CREATIVITY

CHAPTER 1

THE LESSON

One fateful day in middle school, a mean girl changed the trajectory of my life.

I don't remember her name, or even what she said. It doesn't matter, really. What matters is what happened next.

As soon as I got home, I burst into tears, went upstairs, and threw myself on my bed. I was so despondent, I couldn't do my homework. I opened my bedroom door and wailed down at my mom that I wasn't coming down to dinner.

After dinner, there was a knock on my bedroom door. It was Dad.

"Don't come in!" I managed through the sobs.

"When you're ready to talk, I'll be down on the porch," he said.

When the sobbing finally subsided, I took my puffy-faced self down to the porch. Dad put his paper down and asked what had happened at school. I launched into a long explanation of how this girl had wronged me. I went on and on about how mean she was, how she had hurt me for absolutely no reason, how the situation was so unfair.

Dad let me ramble on and on, let me get it all out.

When I was finally done, I expected him to pat me on the shoulder, commiserate about what a horrible person this girl must be, and tell me it would all be better. So what he said next surprised me.

"How do you think she's feeling right now?"

"I don't know, and I don't care!" I said reflexively. "She's so awful! I'm never going near her again!"

And then he surprised me again. He told me to close my eyes.

"What?!"

"Just humor your dad for a minute. Close your eyes." I did as I was told.

"Now, I want you to imagine you are the other girl," Dad said.

"But—" I started to object.

"I mean it. Really think about it. You are her. Her face is your face. Her feelings are your feelings." He paused for a few minutes, giving me time to imagine it.

It took me awhile, but I found my way there. I was her.

"Got it?"

"Yeah."

"Now I want you to replay your entire interaction from today, everything each of you said to each other. But I want you to see it all—feel it all—from her perspective."

And so I did.

And . . . wow.

Just WOW.

Of course that's why she said what she said. She was feeling threatened and hurt and angry. If I'd been her, with her perspective and the situation at hand, I probably would have done exactly the same thing.

And really, none of it had all that much to do with me. I had taken the situation far too personally, and massively overreacted. I was sure I'd hurt her, too. I felt terrible.

How could I have missed it?

I didn't realize it at the time, but Dad had just given me a master class in empathy. I know now, this was the defining lesson of my childhood. The practice of empathy, being willing and able to step into another's shoes, has pushed me past countless boundaries and opened up endless opportunities.

It made me a better friend.

It made me a better writer.

It made me a better negotiator.

It made me a better marketer.

It made me a better mom.

It made me a better community builder.

In fact, I believe this simple lesson is the most important, bedrock principle underlying the brand and global movement that I'm leading today.

So thank you, mean girl, wherever you are. I'm sure you're a very nice person now.

And thank you, Dad. For teaching me the value of empathy. Of learning to pause and take time to really see things from another's point of view. When you start with empathy, life becomes so much bigger and richer. Your creativity flows, not from the head but from the heart. And when it comes from your heart, there's no need to second-guess it. You can trust that it's taking you exactly where you need to go.

CHAPTER 2

THE ORANGUTAN SWEATER

The summer before my junior year of high school, when I was trying to figure out where I might go to college, our family of four made plans to take an epic car trip from my hometown of Tulsa, Oklahoma, to the University of North Carolina, then up the Eastern seaboard where we would visit New York University and Boston University, then spend a few days in Cape Cod before beginning the long journey back home.

The car trip turned out to be memorable in more ways than one.

First, there was the legendary Waffle House Battle, a verbal showdown between my mother and father about where we were going to pull off the highway and eat dinner. In the vitriol that spewed forth about selfishness and commitment and pancakes, it became clear to me and my younger sister that our parents' 24-year marriage was coming to an end.

Then there was the Atlantic City debacle, wherein my father had decided it would be fun to "wing it" and find a place to stay on the spot, rather than letting my mom pre-book a hotel as she had done for all of the other nights of the trip. Turns out, there were three major conventions going on in Atlantic City that night. After trying four separate hotels, we ended up in a room with one double bed for the four of us—a dilemma that Dad "solved" by (quite uncharacteristically) staying out at the casino all night.

But it turns out that, for me anyway, the most memorable moment of the Epic Road Trip of 1984 was when we stopped to visit my parents' longtime friends, Sylvia and Orion Daniel, in Charlotte, North Carolina.

They were a wonderful, welcoming couple, full of Southern charm. Orion had a booming laugh and terrific sense of humor. Sylvia was quick to make us feel at home, and it turned out she was something of an entrepreneur. She asked if we'd like to drive over and check out her "little retail biz."

Sylvia was the proud owner of a yarn shop.

To say I was bored by the time we arrived at Sylvia's is putting it mildly.

We'd long since dispensed with the cute car games that families play at the beginning of a long trip. We'd each sunk into sulky silence, absorbed in our own activities. I'd finished whatever books I'd brought along to read, and the length of the drive, coupled with the tension, had me saying to myself, "Calgon, take me away!"

I was bored. I was anxious. I needed an escape—anything, anything, to distract me from my parents' fighting, my college fears, my racing thoughts. Anything to help me feel calm and centered and productive.

I didn't realize it then, but I had a knitter inside me, just waiting to get out.

Sylvia intuitively recognized this right away. But, like all knitters of some experience, she had learned patience. She knew that, as a 16-year-old wannabe fashionista, I was likely to balk at the thought of what was traditionally seen as an old-fashioned hobby.

So she made us a meal and chatted us up before suggesting the quick side trip to her shop. I was just so happy to be out of that car. How could I say no? We pulled up to her place, and I barely noticed the sign out front—"Knitwits." I was looking up the block, hoping to spot a cute clothing boutique that we could visit, as soon as this was over with.

I remember being intrigued walking into that shop, while still thinking, This obviously isn't for me. Mainly I recall lots of knitted afghans. I reached out to touch some of the yarn, and they all felt either scratchy (wool) or squeaky (acrylic). I looked longingly out the store window, still searching for somewhere else, somewhere trendier to go next.

Then Sylvia uttered, in her charming Charlotte drawl, "Wanna give it a try?"

I looked, and there she was, holding out two very long, pointy plastic sticks, and a big pink roll of yarn.

Blink, blink.

"Me? Oh, I really don't think I can do that."

"Don't be silly; you're such a smart cookie, you'll pick it up quick."

"But aren't I too young to learn? I mean, everything looks so . . . complicated."

"Oh come on, you can do it!" she said, as she thrust the needles into my hands.

"It's really easy, there are just four little steps . . . see . . . under the fence, around the back, back through the fence, off jumps Jack!" As she repeated the silly rhyme, she covered my fingers with her own, making the motions with me. Kind of like when I was first learning to ride a bike, with my dad running alongside me with his hand on the seat as I screamed don't let go, don't let go!

It was methodical. Rhythmic. Somehow comforting.

And then before I knew it, Sylvia's hands weren't there, and I was knitting.

I WAS KNITTING!

I was instantly hooked.

Stitch after stitch, row after row . . . It was so much more satisfying than any other craft I had tried. My mom had tried to get me to needlepoint, but I didn't get the point. How boring was it to see a picture, and cover the picture with colored yarn? It was like painting by numbers.

But this . . . THIS!

Making something where before there was nothing. Creating my own fabric. I was the artist, painting with fiber. And there was something so soothing, so rhythmic about it. Instinctively, I could feel that my brain needed this. It was balanced, it was meditative.

It was magic.

I finally looked up, and Sylvia was beaming. I knew the light in her eyes was reflected in my own. I was a knitter, and there was no turning back.

The day I first learned to knit, at a local yarn store in Charlotte, NC, owned by the late Sylvia Daniel.

The next challenge was for me to find something I really wanted to make.

Sylvia suggested a simple blanket, but I longed to make clothing—something fitted, on-trend, but one-of-a-kind . . . a summer tank top, maybe? I went digging past all the afghan patterns, leafing through all the books, like a mad scientist in search of a secret formula. No luck.

Time was running out—my mom and sister were ready to head back to the car. So I grabbed the next pattern I saw— a cable-knit sweater pattern.

"Hmmm," Sylvia said. "I don't know . . . that's pretty advanced."

"I'm sure I can figure it out!" I said with my newfound confidence. "I've got the whole rest of the trip to make it!" God bless her, Sylvia helped me pick out the right gauge of yarn—the softest skein of pale pink I could find—and I was on my way.

It turned out I'd bitten off a little more than I could chew. When I dropped my first stitch on the way to Atlantic City, I called Sylvia and she did her best to talk me through it. This was long before Ravelry.com, the online pattern hub for knitters. Sylvia was my only "YouTube." I still don't have any idea how she managed to explain—over the phone— how to use a cable hook.

But I was on a roll. Or more accurately, I was riveted. Obsessed. Addicted. In the car, at restaurants, on the beaches of Cape Cod . . . I was never *not* knitting.

And somehow, shortly after returning to Tulsa, I finished my first project—that cabled sweater. I had to admit, it looked pretty amazing.

There was only one problem: The arms were about six inches too long.

It will forever be known as my Orangutan Sweater.

And it's still the best thing I ever made.

Growing up in the 1970s, we were taught that hobbies and business should be separate. Hobby = fun. Business = work. On *Shark Tank*, Mark Cuban is fond of telling aspiring entrepreneurs, "You don't have a business. You have a hobby. I only invest in businesses."

On the other hand, you've probably heard this quote, which has been attributed to everyone from Mark Anthony to Confucius: "Do what you love, and you'll never work a day in your life."

With apologies to all three men, I call B.S. on both of these statements.

Instead, I prefer this quote from singer-songwriter Graham Coxon: "My hobby is my job. It's a jobby!"

When you're lucky enough to find something creative that lights you up inside. Something you know you could do every single day for the rest of your life. Something you're willing to—yes—put in *a ton of work* to grow and build. When you're lucky enough to find your jobby, don't shrink from it. Embrace it. Even if everyone tells you you're crazy. *Especially* if everyone tells you you're crazy.

A jobby is one of the greatest gifts you can give yourself and, more important, that you can give the world. When you have the space to apply deep focus to your passion, to immerse yourself in it and explore and challenge convention and fail and try again, you make discoveries. When you share these discoveries with others in the form of your business, you're not just making a living. You're making little joyful advancements for the whole human race.

This has been true for millennia, from the Greek philosophers to the artists of the Renaissance. And with the current pace of advancements in automation and artificial intelligence, it becomes truer with each passing day. Creativity is the new currency. If you can turn your creativity into your career, you'll have the best possible job security. And even better, you'll have the unmatched thrill of doing what you love while making a lasting impact on the world.

CHAPTER 3

EVERY MOVE THAT COMES BEFORE LAYS THE FOUNDATION

The year before the Epic Road Trip, I got my first real job. (From that day until this, I've never stopped working.)

My parents didn't talk about it, but it was clear that money had gotten tighter at home. I had a strict allowance that barely covered the gas for me to get my mom's old Dodge Omni to school and back each day, let alone go to the movies. Of course, that's not unusual for a teenager, and clearly just the fact that I had a car of any sort made me more privileged than most. But my friends always seemed to have more cash than me. So if I didn't want to miss out on the fun, it was time to join the workforce.

My first job? In a morgue.

By high school, I was pretty sure I wanted to be a professional writer of some sort. So when Mr. Hinkle, my 10th-grade English teacher, revealed he had a weekend side hustle at the *Tulsa World* (our daily paper), and that they might need extra help, I jumped at the chance.

The *Tulsa World* had not yet arrived in the digital age, so they still maintained what dailies called a "morgue." Every day, a morgue worker would perform a sort of autopsy on that day's published paper. He or she would take scissors and cut out each article, one by one, then file them in manila folders of various sizes, depending on the topic. Some files contained only one clipping. Others, like "1984 Memorial Day Flood," were four inches thick.

I was far too young and inexperienced to be a clipper or even a filer.

My sole job was to wait for the phone from the newsroom to ring. When a reporter requested a file, I would locate it and walk it down to the newsroom so they could reference what they needed, and when they were done, I'd walk it back to the morgue.

When I was bored (which was often), I was free to read through the files or do homework.

This seemingly menial job dramatically altered the trajectory of my life.

Up to this point, my dream job had been to become a journalist. I was schlepping files every day to my heroes, the people who were living the life I aspired to live. I had always pictured the big-daily reporters as living incredibly exciting lives—pounding the streets, searching out great stories, uncovering truths—and most of all, delving deep into the backstories and psyches of the world's most fascinating people.

This isn't the life I found in the *Tulsa World* newsroom.

What I found instead was a bunch of really sad-seeming people with downturned mouths, staring morosely at their computers and slugging coffee all day.

They would hardly glance up when I arrived with a file. To be fair, I'm sure my earnest and chipper 16-year-old self was pretty annoying. But still. There was no denying the fact they all had the same pasty, almost greenish skin tone that said, "I never see the sunlight." The lack of passion was palpable.

My bubble was burst.

And this was a tremendous gift.

(Many bursting bubbles are, believe it or not.)

Because I knew that I still wanted to be a writer, just not THIS kind of writer. So I started searching for a field where I could write, but also get out and about to meet new people and learn new things. A job that would really push me. A job that was never the same day twice.

Technical writer? Too boring.

Magazine writer? Too hard to break into, unless you were from New York.

Screenwriter? Also too hard to break into, unless you were from L.A.

Writer writer, like short stories and fiction and nonfiction? "You can't really do that as a job," my teachers and parents explained. "Only a few are lucky enough to do it for a living, and it takes years and years for your first break."

Things were looking pretty grim.

A few months after my *Tulsa World* internship ended, I attended an event put on by the local Chamber of Commerce called "Camp Enterprise." At the time, it seemed like a cool way to get out of school. It turned out to be an incredibly dull two days; speaker after speaker droned on about careers in manufacturing, oil production, accounting.

And then one presenter named Fred took the stage and completely shattered the mold. He explained that he worked at an advertising agency, helping to create ad campaigns for print and video. He was full of energy, and hilarious, and he mesmerized the crowd with his wild tales of no-holds-barred brainstorming sessions and crazy clients and break-neck-paced TV commercial shoots.

He said that what he loved about his job was that it was completely different every day. He got to dive into other people's businesses and figure out how to convey their message to their intended target audience. Every business was different. Every audience was different. Every day was different, uniquely challenging, and creatively rewarding.

Fred called himself a "copywriter."

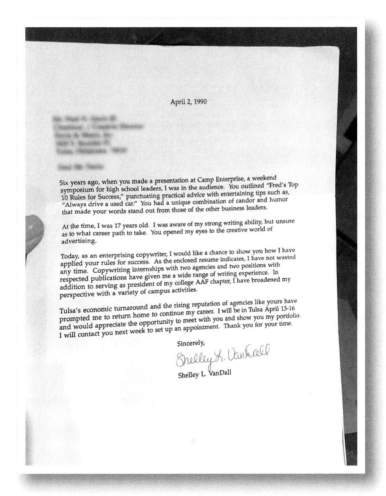

One of many letters sent in the relentless search for internships.

I'd found my new dream.

And so it was that this particular burst bubble was actually a dot in disguise, connecting my childhood dreams of journalism to my future path, and getting me one step closer to fulfilling my true purpose.

CHAPTER 4

THE ART OF THE AD

After the Epic Road Trip, I'd given up the dream of an East Coast school. My parents' impending divorce necessitated that I narrow my list to schools that offered the best chance at a scholarship. I focused on colleges with some type of advertising degree, which further shortened the list. When I was offered a full ride to Texas Christian University, my decision was made—even though this meant I would forever be labeled a Horned Frog.

Naturally, the transition to college life was not without its challenges. TCU seemed to be the land of the beautiful people, where girls put on dresses and makeup and teased their Texas big hair just to go to a football game. My freshman roommate was desperately homesick, which was strange, because she was from Fort Worth (where TCU is located). She left midyear. But by that point, I was settling in, learning to maneuver my advertising major and political science minor classes, grateful (and a little guilty) to be removed from the divorce drama back in Tulsa.

But soon, another challenge loomed: the apparent impossibility of the career I had chosen.

The ad business was big business in those days. It was fast. It was sexy. Everyone wanted in. From the beginning of freshman year, our advertising professors warned us that our best hope out of college was to start out as an intern, fetching coffee. If we worked really hard, after a few years of fetching, we might be able to snag a position as an assistant to the assistant account executive or assistant to the assistant media buyer.

But a job in the creative department?

Forgettaboutit.

Another alarming realization: None of the "advertising" faculty at TCU had actually worked in advertising. There were former journalists and world communication experts, but no former copywriters or creative directors or even account executives.

And while I would receive a really solid grounding in grammar, spelling, and punctuation, along with journalistic principals, any real advertising expertise would have to come from real-world experience.

It was up to me to find it. I needed a summer internship.

Until this point, I'd always held a job—whatever job I could find. From schlepping and pricing Christmas ornaments in a 110-degree warehouse in July to schlepping beer and brats at a popular pub. I'd worked in a dermatologist's office and an ice cream parlor and continued to babysit all the while.

But now it was time to get serious.

Armed with the ignorance of an idealistic college freshman, I pulled out the Tulsa yellow pages and composed cover letters to every company listed under "Advertising Agency," "Design," and "Marketing." In the letters, I explained that I was destined to become a copywriter and I would do any job they needed, if only they would hire me as a summer intern at minimum wage. I mailed off no fewer than two dozen of these letters.

I trudged to my student mailbox every day, hoping for a reply. Nothing. Zero. Zilch.

So next, I picked up the phone. I was sweetly relentless. I called and left messages and called again.

And finally, after weeks of rejection, a woman named Cindy, owner of a tiny boutique design firm, called me back.

She asked if I could drive home for an interview.

I couldn't jump into my car and hop onto Interstate 35 fast enough.

At that first copywriting job, I learned that advertising could actually be tasteful.

In her beautiful, feminine office laden with oriental rugs, rich tapestries, and Asian objets d'art, Cindy preferred to sit at her huge, heavy desk and create ads with a calligraphy pen, rather than at a computer with a mouse.

As the firm's only on-staff copywriter, I was expected to hit the ground running. Which was a challenge. At that point, I hadn't yet had any advertising courses, so I was totally faking it. And Cindy totally knew this—but never said anything. She would just give me a knowing sideways smirk with a smile in her eyes, hand me a handwritten creative brief, and tell me to go to work.

This job was where I first learned the importance of brevity.

To Cindy, copy was a combination of poetry and decoration. I would give her a page full of carefully crafted, persuasive messaging . . . and it would come back with everything crossed out in elegant calligraphy swooshes—save for a single word.

Although hers was just a two-woman shop (plus a couple of freelancers), Cindy had a deeply impressive client list. She was sought out by high-end brands looking for an artistic edge. She had a strong connection to Nashville, where major recording artists often tapped her to design their album covers.

There was also a unique level of freedom. As far as Cindy was concerned, I could come and go as I pleased, as long as the copy got written.

Whenever I could, I would try to get an in-person meeting with the person inside the company who made everything "tick"—sometimes this was the founder, or the C.O.O., or the marketing director, or the musician. If I could somehow get just five minutes and have them share their story with me, I could begin to empathize with the customer's journey, begin to picture myself in their customer's shoes. I could visualize their hopes and dreams, and how the product or service or song might help change their life for the better. And when I could truly understand this underlying story, feel it, *believe* in it, then when I sat down to write with my long legal pad, the copy would seem to write itself.

When that first summer internship came to an end, I knew I had to keep going on this career path. I had a new thirst for stories and the telling that just naturally evolved into selling.

I had fallen—quickly, madly, deeply—in love with this job that never felt like a job. Every day was, indeed, a completely new day. I was obsessed with learning about each new client—their history, their mission, their customers, and their goals. I loved distilling it all down into a few powerful words and beautiful images. There was magic in creating a connection with the customer, through creativity and the shared human experience. And the discovery of this magic, this sharing from a place of empathy, story, and service rather than "selling," would become the secret sauce to my growth and success, not only in my just-beginning ad career, but in all of the crazy twists and turns that lay ahead.

CHAPTER 5

YOU HAVE 1,000 MORE IDEAS IN YOUR HEAD

As I rounded the home stretch toward graduation from TCU, I could feel the panic level rising steadily among my fellow students in the Advertising/Public Relations program. It was the golden age of advertising agencies, the peak before the rapid descent that followed the rise of the web, Facebook, and the iPhone. Ad agency creative directors rode around Dallas in their Bentleys, snorting cocaine with big-haired, doe-eyed supermodels, and dreaming of creating the next big Super Bowl commercial.

It was every college boy's fantasy.

I remember reading in *Adweek* magazine that a survey of the American public placed "ad agency executive" second-to-last on a list of Most Trustworthy Jobs—barely edging out "car dealer" for the dubious distinction of most dishonest careers.

But dang, I still had to admit, it looked exciting.

Unfortunately, in advertising, entry-level jobs were non-existent. Even for a go-getter girl who already had hands-on experience in the field.

Our professors tried to lower our expectations. "Be prepared to take anything you can get," they lectured. "Unpaid internship, coffee-fetcher, janitor. Get a foot in the door any way you can, and after a few years of proving yourself, an assistant sales position might open up."

"But what if we don't want to be in sales?" I'd ask. "What if we want to be in the creative department?" They'd laugh. Then, as they realized I wasn't kidding, the laughter would turn to pity.

"You can't work in the creative department right out of college. It just doesn't happen that way," they'd say.

There was that word again: can't.

Did I really have to take their word for it? How could they be so sure?

So I got out my trusty yellow pages—for Dallas, Fort Worth, and Tulsa—and started calling. I began with the agencies that had big, sleek ads and their names in bold, capital letters, then worked my way down to the quiet, one-liner companies.

I think I contacted more than 50 ad agencies, PR firms, and companies with in-house ad agencies. This was long before LinkedIn and Glass Door, so I also snail-mailed dozens of résumés. Then I called some more. I made note of every human that I got to speak to, carefully recording the spelling of their name and their position. Whenever I got a "no," I asked if they knew any agency that was hiring.

My list continued to dwindle, and the rejections continued to mount. When we were about two months from graduation I spoke with my mom on the phone and told her how none of my classmates had jobs yet, that the market was incredibly tough, and that I was starting to worry I might not have a job when I graduated. "At least I know I can live with you in Tulsa until I find a job, right?" I laughed.

Silence on the other end of the line.

"Um . . . right, Mom?"

Partway through college, my parents' divorce had been finalized. At this point, in 1990, mom had a three-bedroom house and Dad had a tiny one-bedroom apartment. So Mom's house was my logical landing pad.

Finally, Mom spoke up. "Okay, you can live here after college, but only for one month. Then you'll need to find an apartment or something."

Hmm. Just like that, the dichotomy came into sharp focus: Employment. Or homelessness.

Back to the yellow pages I went.

I sat in the middle of the floor of my dorm room, staring at the phone, summoning the courage to re-call the same agencies that had already turned me down. I decided to re-try an unassuming-looking one-liner agency listing in Jenks, Oklahoma, called O'Neil & Associates. The last time I'd called them, they said they already had two copywriters, and didn't need any more. But I'd heard from another agency (after they rejected me) that O'Neil was on the rise, having recently hired a hotshot creative director and having acquired a slew of new accounts.

I took a deep breath, picked up the phone, and punched in the number.

I got the receptionist and asked if Mr. Hotshot was available.

She transferred me, and as I was mentally preparing for the voice mail message I would leave . . .

"Hello?"

Oh sh*t. It was Hotshot.

"Oh, uh . . . hi."

"Who's this?"

"Uh . . . this is Shelley VanDall."

"Well, Shelley VanDall, what do you want?"

"Um uh um uh . . . I'm about to graduate with a degree in Ad/PR from TCU, and I wondered if you might be looking for a copywriter?"

"Ah, a Horny Toad, right? Can you come in Friday?"

"Uh, Horned Frog, yeah. And sure, I can come in Friday."

"See you at 10 A.M."

Hot damn!

When I walked into O'Neil & Associates that Friday, it was a madhouse.

Account executives were waving their arms and bellowing through the halls about deadlines.

Art directors were literally running from the copy machine to their desks and back again.

The atmosphere was positively vibrating with adrenaline and bursts of maniacal laughter, with stress levels bordering on full-blown anxiety disorder.

I loved it.

I *had* to be a part of it.

As the receptionist walked me back toward Hotshot's office, I realized the maniacal laughter was coming from him. He was on the phone, regaling some client with his unique brand of laser-sharp focus coupled with bawdy-bordering-on-inappropriate humor.

As his piercing blue eyes landed on me, he wound up his phone call by saying, "Hey, I've gotta go, I've got a Horned Frog in my office.

"So, you wanna be a copywriter?" he said to me.

"Yes, I mean . . . I kind of already am. I've done a bunch of internships. . . ."

"Let's see your stuff."

I handed him my portfolio. He flipped it open.

"Hmm . . . this one's crap." He turned the pages. "Crap . . . crap . . . total crap."

I could feel the heat rising in my face.

"Well, this one's not too bad. And this one . . . hmm . . ." He looked up at me.

"With some real direction, and a decent art director, there might be hope for you yet." And then he offered me the job.

"You'll make twelve thousand dollars a year to start. I hope you like to eat ramen noodles."

It was a ridiculously low salary. He knew it. I knew it. And still to this day, it's the most satisfying deal I've ever made. It meant that I had chosen the right career path. It meant that somebody—a highly regarded established somebody—believed in my creativity and was willing to make a long-term investment in me.

Working at O'Neil & Associates was exactly the adrenaline rush I hoped it would be.

On the very first day, Hotshot showed me to my tiny desk in the middle of the traffic department—the chaotic hub of an agency that was responsible for keeping the projects moving and ensuring all deadlines are met. The agency had grown far faster than anyone expected, and the result was a jungle of hurriedly added office furniture, crammed wall to wall in every common space.

I sat down at my desk with the job ticket that Hotshot had handed me. My first real job ticket as a full-time employee!

It was to write a radio commercial for a car dealership. Not quite the glamorous first assignment I had hoped for, but I knew I had to start somewhere. So I put on my empathetic writing hat and thought back to how I had felt when I bought my first new car. The words flowed onto my little PC. After an excessive number of revisions, I timidly approached Hotshot's office with my copy.

"Not bad," he said. "Not great either, so don't go getting a big head . . . but not bad."

I kept my poker face, thanked him, and when I was safely out of his office, did a little dance down the hallway back to my desk.

I started to get more and more assignments—mostly for car dealer ads, which seemed to be an O'Neil specialty. The agency's client list was growing fast, and we had just three writers on staff—Hotshot, me, and a woman who was almost never in the office. She seemed really funny and bright, but I think she had been working there before Hotshot was brought on and now felt displaced by the new Wild West, fast-and-furious vibe of the place. I was bummed, because I had looked forward to being mentored by what was, at the time, a most exotic and rare specimen: a female creative director.

Then one day, a new job ticket arrived on my desk—and it *wasn't* a car dealer spot! It was for a small regional bank. And it wasn't just an ad or a radio script. They wanted a *tagline*. This was big-time. This was the copywriter's equivalent of developing a company's logo. Hotshot must have really believed in me to entrust me with such a big task!

With all the enthusiasm of a naïve 20-something, I dove into my research. I filled three pages on my yellow legal pad—single-spaced—with potential taglines. I circled, I scratched out, I wrote some more. Finally, I narrowed it down to three, with my favorite at the top of the page, and approached Hotshot's office.

He looked it over. Looked up at me over his glasses. Got up from his chair, walked out from behind his desk and past me, shut the door, and returned to his desk. I was so confident in my amazing tagline, I assumed he was about to lavish me with praise and didn't want the others to hear.

"So your best tagline is this one, huh?" he began. I nodded eagerly.

"'Big enough to bank on, small enough to care'?" he said. Somehow, when I heard him read the tagline, it didn't seem so brilliant.

"Um, yeah. What do you think?"

"Shelley, I think you've got 1,000 more ideas in your head, just waiting to come out."

"But . . . but . . . I thought it was so perfect. It says exactly what makes the bank special. It's true. It's real."

"It's TRITE. It's been done a million times. You just don't realize it because you're so new to all of this. Some of it just comes with time."

"But, but . . ." Sigh. "Okay."

It felt like he was being unreasonably tough on me. I fought back tears.

"Go fill another three pages in that yellow legal pad of yours," he said gently. "I know you've got it in you."

Well, at least he didn't think I was a lost cause.

As I walked back to my desk, head bowed, I realized: I still had a long way to go. Just because my creativity had been validated by getting this job, that didn't mean there wasn't more to learn. Every day would mean a new ad. A new *challenge*. Still to this day, when writer's block strikes, I hear Hotshot in my head: "A thousand more ideas."

I turned my legal pad to a fresh sheet of paper and began again.

Eventually, I convinced Hotshot that I needed to move out of the "pit" workspace that the traffic department and most of the other departments' younger staff shared, and into my own office. I explained that, while I loved brainstorming in groups, I needed a quiet space to do my thinking and writing. The tiniest distraction was like someone yelling "SQUIRREL!" and I found myself having to start, start, and restart every project.

Finally, Hotshot was able to move me to a tiny, broom-closet-size office near the receptionist's desk. Compared to the chaos of the pit, this was bliss.

One day, I was happily humming along on some long-form copy for a healthcare brochure. It was a relatively straightforward job, so I'd left my door open.

I heard Hotshot's booming voice coming off the elevator into the lobby, along with another male voice I didn't recognize. Together, they rounded the corner and walked past my office, turning down the next hallway and talking about the framed ads hanging on the wall.

Something hit me in a flash.

Hit me hard.

That's the guy you're going to marry.

Say whaaaaat, inner voice?

This made no sense.

But the feeling was loud, insistent. Palpable.

That's him. That's the guy.

At the time, I was dating another guy, pretty seriously. We'd been together more than a year, and now that we were both settling down with "real" jobs, we had begun to talk tentatively about the future. But now, here was this voice in my head.

As I sat there, knocked off balance and wondering what it meant, Hotshot and Mystery Guy came walking back down the hall. Turns out, Mystery Guy's name was Brent Brander. Brent was an art director from a competing agency and, Hotshot said, if he got his way, Mr. Brander would be joining our agency immediately.

Brent and I smiled and greeted each other, and then they walked out to the elevators.

Whoa.

Later that day around the water cooler, the new art director was the hot topic. Someone mentioned that he was 32. And married.

Double whoa.

Clearly, my intuition had been WAY off. I immediately put any romantic notion about Brent out of my mind. I felt silly and girlish for having had the thought in the first place.

From the next week forward, Hotshot paired Brent and me as creative partners. It turned out we were a natural creative team. Brent's visual ideas would prompt my words, and vice versa. We would sit for hours, alternatively talking about the ad challenge at hand, then joking around and talking about random stuff—pop culture, politics, family, life. It's how we got into the creative zone. At the least expected times, inspiration would always strike. Hours would tick by, unnoticed, as new ad ideas bloomed into fruition.

Every day at 3 P.M., it was "treats time." The creatives would form a single-file line and traipse along the two-lane road a few blocks to the Apco station, where we would carb load to get a creative second wind and continue churning out ads well past sunset. I noticed that Brent usually got a PAYDAY bar, with the rare exception of ROLOs instead.

I was starting to notice more little things about Brent.

And our coworkers were starting to notice Brent and me, noticing each other.

More and more of the projects on the Job List started to have the same initials in the Writer and Art Director columns: SV and BB. And yet somehow, it never entered my mind, after that first "flash" encounter, that Brent might have the slightest interest in me. He was *married*. He was *old and wise*—an ancient 32! I was a *baby,* fresh out of school, fully immersed in my career, fully focused on earning Hotshot's approval for one ad after the next, working toward my goal of moving from copywriter to associate creative director—someday.

Someday was about to arrive, much faster than anyone expected—least of all, me.

CHAPTER 6

MY OWN SHINGLE

As often happened with ad agencies in the '90s, O'Neil & Associates quickly reached its peak, and began to decline. Unbeknownst to most of us, an embezzlement scandal was brewing, involving the office manager and several of her family members that worked at the agency. The leaders of the agency, including Hotshot, were in the office less and less. Then, Brent left to start his own design firm. Something was telling me it was time to move on. So, when I got a chance to interview with Tulsa's biggest agency, Advertising Incorporated, I jumped at the chance.

While Ad Inc might not have had the most imaginative name or sexiest working environment (the offices looked more like a 1950s insurance agency than a hot ad shop), my time there did provide me with two very valuable gifts.

The first was that I learned to work with large corporate clients, and still find a way to inject creativity and fun into the messaging. We took a dry, bland, public utility account—Oklahoma Natural Gas—and created campaigns with humor and relatable life situations, and even got our spokesperson to jump out of an airplane. This led to lots of awards and accolades and increased sales for the clients. Best of all, I started to work my way out of the back room into the client meetings, where I learned to lobby for my own creative concepts and form strategic partnerships with the clients as we endeavored to refine the messaging together.

The second gift of Ad Inc was one of my greatest lifelong mentors—a five-foot-tall powerhouse in four-inch stiletto heels named Dorcas Meroney. A senior account executive, Dorcas modeled for me how to interact successfully with the male leadership of the agency. She was brilliant, with a razor-sharp wit and flawless intuition. She spoke her mind, clearly and unapologetically. And she could deftly handle inappropriate or sexist remarks, cutting them off at the pass without incident or repercussions.

Dorcas consistently championed me, getting me assigned to her accounts whenever she could, getting me invited into client meetings, and encouraging me to take chances with my creativity.

Most important, when I came to Dorcas and told her I was thinking of leaving Ad Inc to hang out my own shingle, she didn't fire me. On the contrary, she gave me exactly the lift I needed to make it happen.

Shortly after Brent left O'Neil to start his own design firm, he and his first wife decided to divorce. Eventually, inevitably, we had begun to date. I spent a lot of time at his office, as he burned the midnight oil to meet his deadlines. And I was jealous. I loved the idea of controlling my own schedule, my own destiny. Not having to answer to anyone. Not having to deal with sexist coworkers. Not having to defend my creative concepts to a slew of account executives just to get them out the door and in front of the client. With each passing day, I was more distracted by my inner voice saying, *NOW. Now is the time to go out on your own.*

Finally one day, I got up the guts to head into Dorcas's office. After all the time and generosity that she'd put into mentoring me, I really dreaded telling her that I was thinking of leaving. I pictured her bounding up from behind her desk and escorting me straight out of the building to my car.

So it was a complete and utter shock when she said, "Oh my God, I am *so excited* for you. I am *so proud* of you. And your timing is perfect."

Um . . . what? Was she being sarcastic? What was going on?

Dorcas proceeded to swear me to silence, then shared that Ad Inc was planning to close by the end of the year. Too many major clients had left, and the C.E.O. was tired of trying to keep the doors open. "So I'm thinking between now and then, we can let you handle the Oklahoma Natural Gas account on a freelance basis. That will give you a great head start with some consistent income. I'll need to talk to the client, but I'm pretty sure she'll go for it," she said.

This was the kind of gift horse you didn't look in the mouth.

Within a month from that day, I'd opened my first business. I called it Copy Café. At the age of 25, I was an entrepreneur. Copywriter, creative director, and account executive—all in one. Oh, and don't forget accountant, production assistant, office manager, and toilet cleaner!

The challenge of it all was so exhilarating. Every day was wildly different. No one was looking over my shoulder. No more job tickets or change orders. I could stay in my apartment and write in my pajamas all day if I wanted to! But I never did. I woke up before dawn each morning, too excited to see where the next day would take me.

Even at 25, I knew. I would never work for anyone else again.

I was an entrepreneur for life.

I set up shop in an office-for-rent building, right next door to Brent's business, One Brander Creative (1 B.C.), and across the hall from Hotshot—who by now, had opened his own firm as well. The old band was back together—but this time, we each controlled our own destiny. It was the perfect situation for a bunch of crazy creative types. We could come together, hang out and brainstorm, then retreat to our own corners to write and design for our own clients.

Over time, I was coming to realize that the ad biz, with all its glitz and glam, was not for the faint of heart. Clients can be fickle. You're always one account away from making or breaking your year. In a larger company, there's a never-ending, unspoken battle between the creatives and the account executives. The creatives think all the AEs are sellouts with zero creative integrity, who only care about sales. The AEs think the creatives are fragile flowers, weirdos, or both—artsy types who are just looking to make pretty ads and only care about awards that feed their boundless egos.

In my years working at agencies, I saw and heard it all. Creatives stealing credit for each other's ideas. Junior AEs stabbing each other in the back to curry favor with senior AEs. Everyone mercilessly making fun of clients. Agencies padding the hours, fabricating bills that didn't exist, undercutting vendors. Everyone throwing everyone under the bus. And the tougher the industry got, as it moved out of the anything-goes 1980s into the more realistic '90s with clients expecting to see more data and research, the more political it got inside those agency doors.

Neither Brent nor I were ever really cut out for the corporate agency life. We were both in it for the love of the ad itself. For using words and type and pictures to stop someone, get their attention, maybe make them smile or laugh . . . and then help them solve a genuine problem. We knew that a good ad—a great ad—could actually make people's lives better.

We lived in a constant chase for those moments.

Late at night, there was anxiety about work, for each of us. Would we ever achieve enough stability in this business, alone or together? Would we forever be locked in a vicious battle of pitches—for the next ad, the next account, the next client?

I once heard someone compare the ad agency creative life to a classic Looney Tunes cartoon. You're Wile E. Coyote and the anvil is the next creative assignment, the next deadline, always hanging over your head, suspended in midair, just waiting to fall and crush you. And yet, and yet . . . there's a thrill to the chase. The struggle to find just the right idea out of the 1,000 ideas in your head. The continual up-leveling as you take in feedback—from colleagues, clients, customers—and use it as fuel to make the message stronger. And the joy when that idea really lands, makes someone laugh, touches them deeply, or leads them to a solution that improves their life.

I believe that all creatives struggle on some level with their own anvil. But as you progress in your journey, you can learn to respect and even appreciate the tension it represents. You learn to push past that first idea, to see feedback as an opportunity rather than a failure. You're circling in, learning to trust yourself. Edging ever closer to your own true voice.

CHAPTER 7

THE BRANDERS, THE BEE, AND THE BIG PIVOT

In 1994, after dating for almost four years, Brent and I got married. But I don't think anyone would call what we did "settling down."

Becoming Mrs. Brent Brander, October 1994.

First, we decided that now that we'd merged our lives, it was time to merge our businesses. It would make everything simpler, tax-wise, and we could take advantage of the fact that, right around this time, a trendy new term had begun to emerge as the replacement for the industry previously known as "advertising."

The fancy new word? Branding.

Brent and I joke that, with a name like Brander, we were destined for either ranching or advertising. And neither of us had the heart to poke animals with hot sticks.

After some playing around with combining our company names, Copy Café and One Brander Creative (1B.C.), we landed on Branders Creative Café, Inc. Clever, right? Just one problem: From the day we incorporated, the I.R.S. couldn't seem to understand that we weren't a restaurant. Each month they would write to us, asking why we weren't declaring tip income. So before too long, we settled into a shortened version of the name: Branders, Inc.

Right after combining our business and "re-branding" as Branders, Inc., we had a flood of new clients. Everybody loves a love story. Clients were intrigued by a young husband-and-wife creative team. And at this point, the two of us had each earned a reputation for creative that stood out and got results.

But when we would dream together about the kind of agency we wanted to build we always came up against the same concern. We both dreaded the idea of getting so big that we would just be managers, and we wouldn't get to write or design anything. I thought back to my agency days, the way I'd had to fight my way into those client meetings— and how much more gratifying it was to be able to own the whole process, from customer research, through concept, all the way to execution.

So from the beginning, we made a promise to each other. Branders, Inc. would never be big—at least not in the traditional sense. We would get a pretty new office space where we would be inspired to brainstorm, a place that would lend us more legitimacy with clients than our current rooms. But we would never, ever have more than one employee—a receptionist/office manager. We would never become a mega-agency. We would be first, last, and always, 100 percent about the creative.

We didn't let the dust settle on the family front, either. Within a few months after the wedding, I was pregnant with our son, Sam. Just 16 months after that, our daughter, Cecily came along. And three years later, our second daughter, Mallory.

In the early days of raising my kids, my passion for knitting had a resurgence.

Maybe it was the nesting. Maybe it was my anxiety that needed soothing. Maybe it was the appeal of making something tiny and adorable that went from cast-on to bind-off lickety-split—the near-instant gratification of a baby hat or cardigan.

Somehow, in the three crazy years from when I got pregnant with Sam to when I gave birth to Cecily, I started and finished more sweaters (albeit tiny ones) than in any other period of time, before or since.

I even knit while in labor. In fact, I finished a sweater for Cecily during the 24-plus hours I was birthing her. It was a fantastic distraction! Brent loves to talk about what a waste it was to go through all that Lamaze training, getting careful instruction on how to soothe and support me while in labor—cool washcloths for my face, massaging my shoulders, rubbing my feet. But during each birth, when push came to shove (literally!), I pushed and shoved him away and reached for my knitting needles instead.

Early sweaters made for my three kids.

The repetitive motion of the needles and the tactile feedback of the fiber was like meditation for me—all the way up to the final moment, when I was dilated to 10, my epidural had run out, and they discovered that 10-pound 8-ounce Cecily was "sunny side up" and would need to be manually turned over before she could be delivered.

Even knitting was not enough to get me through those 10 minutes.

Recently, when I pulled out those first tiny sweaters and really examined them, I saw that the knitting was horrendous. I didn't have anyone to teach me the ins and outs of stranded colorwork, intarsia, or cables. There was still no Ravelry, no YouTube, no Knit Stars. But I did have my friend

Kristy, who was into making baby sweaters too. She was a better knitter than me, and lightning-fast.

Kristy's mother, Barbie, was our go-to guru when we got ourselves into a mess. Barbie was also my mom's best friend, so I'd spent a lot of time at her house growing up. She was like a second mom to me. But still, I hated having to call Barbie at 10 o'clock at night, when my dropped stitches always seemed to happen. And in many cases, it couldn't be worked out over the phone (since of course we didn't have FaceTime yet either), necessitating an in-person visit. Which seemed like such a huge imposition. So I usually just worked through the mistakes as best I could and moved on.

That devil-may-care approach to my knitting is undeniably evident in those early baby sweaters. But you know how when you buy a sweater and it has one of those tags that says something like "the inconsistencies in this garment are part of the beauty of a one-of-a-kind, handmade piece"? My knitting was just like that! And nobody can deny that I made each piece my own, in my own wonky little way.

Still, I knew there was a lot to learn, a lot I could improve.

I would need help—guidance, structure, resources—and someone with *loads* of patience. But as a mom of two babies with a booming branding business, I didn't have a lot of time to browse in yarn stores. Still, I couldn't seem to stay away from them.

No matter how old-fashioned, no matter how hopelessly cluttered—there was something magical about yarn stores. The explosion of color. The irresistible tactile-ness of the fiber. The utter improbability that you could click two sticks together and form fabric out of thin air. The endless creative possibilities of taking a pattern, mixing up the yarns, and making a piece of *clothing* that was unlike any other in the whole wide world. A true original.

To my knowledge, there was only one independent yarn store in Tulsa, Oklahoma, in the early 2000s. It was called Needlework Creations, and compared to the big-box chain stores, it was paradise. Instead of aisle after aisle of Hobby Lobby acrylic afghan yarn that squeaked like nails on a chalkboard when you tried to knit with it, this charming little shop had natural fibers, wool from France, alpaca from Peru, and even a small section of yarn that had been hand-dyed by artisans, hank by hank.

Best of all, if I messed up or dropped a stitch, the nice ladies at Needlework Creations would actually help me. I would come in, sheepishly, with my tangled messes. The elegant owner, named Jan, and one of her younger employees (also named Jan), would spot me right away, smile kindly, and shepherd me to the table where they would patiently guide me through fixing the mistake, no matter how monstrous it might be. This was a revelation.

Unlike the big-box craft department manager who just gave me a blank stare, Jan and Jan took the time to "teach the fisherman to fish." I began to understand the anatomy of the stitch. How each stitch was connected to its neighbor to its right, to its left, to the ones above and below.

Just like people, I thought.

At Needlework Creations, I also fell in love—from afar—with my first celebrity knitwear designer, Debbie Bliss, and her sophisticated baby sweater patterns. I was always asking Owner Jan to special-order Debbie Bliss yarn for me. I wanted the exact colors of the exact yarns in the pattern, usually cotton in 10 different colors! Without ever complaining, Jan would do it.

It took several of these orders for Jan to finally, gently explain that she was having to order a full bag of 10 balls of each color, and then getting stuck with the 90 balls left over! I was horrified. I made a point to buy up a bunch of her in-stock yarns, to make up for my obliviousness.

The lesson that Jan taught me, in her most gracious and accommodating way, was that we as consumers can so easily be myopic about our own needs, without pausing to think about the impact on the small business. Working in the service industry is tough. When you've worked as a waiter or waitress, you tip well the rest of your life. When you've worked in retail, you take time to smile and be patient with salespeople. And once you've owned a business, you have a whole new appreciation for the crazy dance—the buying, the selling, the hiring, the firing, the early mornings and sleepless nights.

But until you've lived it, you don't know what you don't know.

So at this point, thanks to Needlework Creations and Jan and Jan, my knitting really took off. I knit at my kids' soccer practice, in doctor's waiting rooms, in the early mornings before the rest of the family opened their eyes. It was my therapy, my sanity, my escape. Every family member and friend received a handmade scarf or hat for Christmas.

Then one day, I bopped into Needlework Creations and Owner Jan called me over. "I have a little sad news," she said. "I'm going to be closing the shop."

I felt like someone had just unplugged my knitting life support.

"Whaaaaat?" I gasped.

"My husband is retiring, and he's always wanted to live in Greece. So we're going to give it a try."

"Oh NO! You can't do that!" I blurted out, then caught myself. "I mean, er . . . I'm really happy for you but . . . I just don't know where I'll go for yarn and for help." I felt the panic rising in my chest. What would I do now?

Jan reached for my hand.

"You know, Shelley, you're so young and you've got so much energy," she said. "You could open your own shop."

I laughed out loud. Hard.

Then I saw that she was serious, and that maybe I'd hurt her just a little bit. So I rambled.

"Oh . . . that's really kind of you to say . . . but I could *never*," I replied, honestly shocked at her suggestion. "I have two kids under four. I have a branding business with my husband, and it's *insane* . . . We do all the advertising for Cox Cable and Cherokee Casinos and Mazzio's . . . I've got three kids under five . . . I work every spare second and barely sleep at all . . . of course it would be a dream but there's *no possible way*. Fun idea but . . . I'll just have to cross my fingers that someone else will do it!"

Jan smiled and said, "Just think about it."

I smiled back and hugged her, thanking her for all her help and wishing her all the best in Greece.

Somewhere deep inside, a seed had been planted.

For a while after Needlework Creations shut its doors, I just went back to knitting at home, alone, using the stash of yarn I'd already built up. But whenever I would pull my needles out, I couldn't help it—daydreams of owning my own yarn shop would emerge, bubbling up into my consciousness.

Just imagine . . . no more writing copy in an effort to sell a client's product—cable TV or pizza or casinos. No more being driven by someone else's deadlines. I could build my *own* brand, be my own client, with no one else editing my copy, no "approval process"! I could fully immerse myself in my weird little passion and introduce a whole new generation to the joys of knitting. I could build something different, something the world needed, a more modern yarn store, a brand. Something I might be able to pass on to my children.

Oh, how amazing it would be to have a jobby!

And then I would stop myself. *Ludicrous*, I thought. *You know nothing about retail. Nothing about inventory. Where would you even begin?*

Eventually, after Needlework Creations closed, I started to run low on yarn. I was itching for a new project. Then I heard from a friend that the local, upscale needlepoint store on Lewis had just added knitting supplies! Maybe they would have classes, too!

I could barely contain myself. The very next day, I decided to squeeze in a trip to this shop, after preschool pickup. This would mean I'd have all three kids in tow. But surely, I reasoned, a craft shop would welcome kids? Chances are it would be run by some affable grandmothers, right?

Ohhhhh, so wrong.

I walked into the needlepoint store ("and knitting!" declared the temporary sign), and as the bell on the door tinkled, I heard a faint shuffling. But I didn't see anyone at the front counter, and no one called out a greeting. I struggled to get through the door with Mallory's infant carrier, and still keep hold of Sam's hand. When we made it through, I set down the carrier, looked up to see cubbies full of yarn, and felt a huge smile begin to form on my face . . .

. . . until I looked to the middle of the store, where I saw THE TABLE.

A group of four women sat there, staring at me. They had all stopped their knitting mid-stitch. After what felt like the world's longest, most awkward pause, the woman I quickly ascertained to be the Queen Bee took long, meaningful glances at each of my children, sizing them up, one by one. I wasn't feeling the warm fuzzies I had hoped for.

Then the Queen Bee spoke, slowly, as if I were a child myself. "Can we help you?" she asked, in that special, disingenuous way that tells you the salesperson, unequivocally, has zero desire to actually help you.

I felt my smile fading, my bubble bursting.

"Um, yes, I was just really excited to hear that you'd opened, I mean, that you'd added yarn, and it's . . . it's beautiful," I stammered, looking at the other women, hoping one would speak up.

Queen Bee glanced at her tablemates, then said, skeptically, "Oh. Do you knit?" The other ladies smirked at one another. I felt my defenses rise.

"Yes. YES, I do. I've knit since I was sixteen years old."

Still, Queen Bee made no move to get up from the table. "Okay then, look around. But *please* keep a close eye on your children. We don't really allow children in here."

Oh . . . okay.

I felt the heat of shame rise to my cheeks, and all I wanted to do was bolt for the door. But I thought of other young moms, like me, and decided to stay as long as I could, to make a point. I looked through all of the yarn, which was mostly overpriced, novelty yarns meant for scarves. Textured yarns such as eyelash and fur were peaking in popularity at that time. I was more interested in sweaters, but the yarn they stocked was scratchy wool, and they were lacking sufficient sweater quantities in most of their colors.

I tried to look through some pattern leaflets and books, but the pictures were uninspiring—mostly poorly lit, cheesy photos of older women in fluffy eyelash scarves. And the patterns were in a completely separate area from the yarns. So, without knowing the store's inventory, and without a good understanding of the principles of yarn substitution, I was really at a loss to pair a pattern with a yarn that I liked.

After a half hour or so, Mallory started to whimper a little bit. It was close to feeding time. I looked up to find the Table Ladies staring at me, mouths turned down in disapproval. I turned to leave, empty-handed and deflated. As

I walked out the door, above the jingling string of bells, I heard them start whispering:

".. . can't believe she'd bring a toddler in here."

".. . too young to be a *real* knitter."

".. . ridiculous!"

My cheeks were on fire. But another fire had started—in my gut.

Nobody deserved to be treated this way. Every knitter, every crocheter, every creative person deserved to be seen, valued, encouraged. Frazzled young moms, working women, busy teens, vibrant retirees, people of all backgrounds and colors and creeds—everyone deserved a chance to learn this craft and blossom and grow.

That day I decided: The world needed a more modern yarn store. A modern yarn movement.

And I was going to be the one to start it.

CHAPTER 8

THE CASHMERE SCARF

I knew exactly where I wanted to open my modern yarn store: in Utica Square, the nicest, most historic shopping center in town. It was a charming, open-air center with a great mix of local boutiques and restaurants, anchored by high-end brands like Saks Fifth Avenue. And there was one small space available that would be perfect for a yarn shop.

I would drive by daily and stare wistfully at the store windows, which were papered with a step-and-repeat message in green: "Something new . . . coming soon to Utica Square" it promised, along with an illustration of the center's famous clock tower.

I'd heard it was impossible to get into Utica Square, which was owned by Walt Helmerich III, the billionaire owner of Helmerich & Payne, an international drilling company. Word on the street was that Utica Square was Walt's "baby." According to legend, Walt, who was then in his 70s, insisted on trimming every tree himself. For locals to get a lease, they needed to know the Helmerichs personally. I was told by more than one person that I needed to adjust my expectations, and consider a cheaper, more attainable location.

"But I've heard that Walt's wife is a knitter!" I would always enthuse. "And I just can't imagine my store anywhere else."

It had to be Utica Square.

So, once the business plan was ready, I marched it into the Utica Square leasing office, bright-eyed and full of hope, and energetically requested to meet with Mr. Helmerich.

The receptionist looked at me, amused but kind. "I'll pass your proposal on to one of our leasing agents," she said.

The next day, I called to inquire, but there was no progress. "I'm sure someone will be back with you soon," they said.

So a few days later, I called back. Same response.

A week later, I called again. Same.

As the weeks passed, I stayed busy with the kids and the business. But the lease proposal was always in the back of my mind. Every time the phone rang, my hopes raised—only to be dashed.

Months passed.

I tried again. This time, I got through to a leasing agent, Jessica.

"Yes, Mr. Helmerich has reviewed your proposal," she said. "He says it looks very interesting, and might be a good fit for Utica Square, but we just don't have an appropriate space available at this time. Please check back in a few months."

Confused, I drove by my dream space, thinking it must have been leased. It still had the "Coming Soon" paper up. *Maybe Jessica just didn't have the heart to kill my dream*, I thought. *Maybe they just think it's a stupid idea.*

But still, I couldn't let it go.

Meanwhile, life was getting even busier. The branding business was more hectic than ever. Sam and Cecily started a new preschool, Undercroft Montessori School, where my sister-in-law, Katy, had been teaching for decades. Mallory was toddling all over the place.

I was still knitting. Still dreaming.

Every few months, I would call Jessica, asking if anything had changed. "Thanks for checking in, but there's no news. We'll call you if something opens up."

Each time, I would drive by my dream space. Paper still up. No change.

By Thanksgiving Day, 2004, I was nearing the end of my rope. Branders business had reached a fever pitch. I was working 10, 12, 14 hours a day. And the wilder things got, the more I couldn't stop thinking about the yarn store. I'd started looking for more storefronts, but I couldn't shake the idea that it needed to be in Utica Square. I was at an impasse.

I decided to throw a Hail Mary. To give it one last shot. And if that didn't work, it was time to move on.

I ordered 100 percent cashmere yarn from a store I'd read about in New York. It was a beautiful, classic gray. The yarn arrived, and with Christmas fast approaching, I knitted an intricate, masculine, cabled scarf. The kind of scarf I imagined a billionaire oil baron might wear.

I then gift-wrapped it, slowly, beautifully, immaculately.

I asked around and found out that Mr. and Mrs. Helmerich lived in a high-rise condo adjacent to Utica Square. The penthouse suite.

Feeling like a bit of a stalker, but determined to give it one last college try, I typed a personal letter to Mr. Helmerich. In the end, it was short and to the point. The world needed a better yarn store, it said. A modern, inspiring store where you could find everything from more affordable yarn all the way up to 100 percent cashmere. The world needed Loops. And it needed to be in Utica Square.

I signed it with a flourish. Folded it, sealed it, attached it to the package.

By now, it was Christmas Eve. Full of the wonder and the hope of the season, I drove to the high-rise condo, marched in, and handed my beautiful package to the doorman. I explained that it was a personal gift, and would he please make sure it was delivered to Mr. Helmerich? He smiled, clearly amused, and promised to make it happen.

As I turned to leave, I was filled with a sense of calm.

I'd done everything I could possibly do.

Whatever happened from this point, it was out of my hands.

The day after New Year's, 2005, my phone rang. It was Jessica.

"I have good news," she said. "Mr. Helmerich is pleased to offer you a lease in Utica Square."

That cashmere scarf taught me a critical lesson that's stayed with me through every challenge since. When you feel something in your gut that you just can't seem to let go of. No matter how strange. No matter how many people say it will never work. When that little voice in your head won't stop whispering, urging you forward. When it's the first thought you awaken to, day after day.

Don't stop.

Tap into your strength—your creativity—and make your move. Make your own version of that cashmere scarf. Take that chance. It's always, always worth it.

Even if I hadn't gotten that lease deal, I'd at least know I'd given it every last stitch of my effort. I'd know I'd put a little more warmth and kindness out into the world. And then I could move forward.

CHAPTER 9

NICENESS AS A U.S.P.

With the opening day of Loops rapidly approaching, my first employee, Emma, and I made a last-minute decision to attend our first trade show—The National Needlearts Association show, held that year in Columbus, Ohio. Neither of us had ever been to a yarn show, and we had no idea what to expect. In my ignorance, I put us on a madcap schedule, flying into Cincinnati and renting a car to drive to Columbus on day one, shopping the entire show on day two, and then driving/flying back home on day three.

I'll never forget that first morning of our first trade show. Emma and I were at the doors to the convention hall, bright and early. A crowd began to gather, and as I looked around, I realized I stood out like a young thumb. Everyone around me was about twice my age and swathed in multiple layers of spectacular hand-knits—many of them, literally, from head to toe. As I pondered the total number of hours that had gone into these women's projects, I was jarred from my reverie by a loud demand.

"My watch says nine o'clock. Open the doors!" yelled one of the attendees near me. *Yelled.*

"YEAH! What's the holdup?!"

"Let's go, buddy!"

The crowd pressed forward. It was like we were at some crazy fiber concert. Emma and I glanced at each other. She looked afraid. What had we signed up for? All I could think was, *Well, Queen Bee's not the only mean one! And if this is what most yarn store owners are like, I've got a real opportunity here.*

In marketing, there's a common term called U.S.P.— Unique Selling Proposition. It's the unique benefit you offer, the attribute that most helps you stand out from your competitors. And, right there on the trade show floor, it suddenly became very clear for me what the U.S.P. for Loops might be.

I could be nice.

In an industry that appeared to be dominated by grumpy women who preferred to run each other over rather than hold the door open . . . who would rather lord their expertise over their customers rather than lift them up . . . I could be nice. I could collaborate. I could connect. I could serve. And in this way, I could stand out.

Suddenly, the doors opened. Emma and I were carried along by the crowd, squished together like bugs. As people began to spread out, all of the possibilities unfolded before us, booth after booth of beautiful yarns and finished objects.

We rushed through that trade show like two kids in the world's biggest candy store. We couldn't get enough—and we were completely overwhelmed. The vendors quickly spotted the ribbons hanging off of our badges that proclaimed: NEW BUYER. They should've said FRESH MEAT! We wrote orders so fast, our wrists ached. We didn't eat. We forgot to drink water. I think Emma had three or four espressos. And when the voice finally came over the loudspeakers to announce that the show was closing for the day, it was like the final bell ringing at the end of a televised fight. We retreated, exhausted, to our own corners in our hotel, and collapsed for the night. Dreams of colorful yarns and spectacular sweaters and ringing cash registers filled my sleep.

It had been hard, but it had all been worth it. I had a fistful of orders placed. And I had my U.S.P.

CHAPTER 10

SWIMMING TOWARD THE BLUE WATER

We opened the first Loops on June 16, 2005. It was Emma's birthday.

It was a "soft" opening—really, really soft. Just a handful of customers trickled in. But that was okay, because we weren't looking for a stampede. We were watching the customers' reactions. And clearly, they were wowed by the merchandising and the branding, with our signature "Loops blue" tying all the graphics and signage together.

"Oh my gosh . . . I've died and gone to yarn heaven."

"Is this a chain? Everything looks so professional."

"Y'all are so nice and helpful."

"I've always dreamed of a place like this."

At that point, I'd never heard of *Blue Ocean Strategy*, the book by W. Chan Kim and Renée Mauborgne that had been published the year before. The idea is to develop an uncontested market space by creating and then capturing new demand. So while all the other "sharks" are fighting each other in the existing market space, turning the ocean red . . . you're always swimming toward the blue ocean where you can differentiate your brand.

In creating that first Loops location, I intuitively swam for the Blue Ocean.

Loops had a number of things that set it apart from all the other yarn stores I'd visited. First, there was a ton of seating: a big sectional sofa, a smaller game table and chairs, barstools around the checkout counter, and a huge community table toward the back. We wanted to send a clear signal that this was a place to come and hang out, to make friends, to form real connections.

Second, there were two swift-and-winder setups for winding yarn. I had read a lot of yarn store reviews over the years, and one of the biggest complaints was about yarn stores that refused to wind your yarn.

For the uninitiated, let me explain: Yarn can be packaged in many different shapes. The traditional "donut" and "bullet" shapes are pre-wound, meaning you can just grab the end and start knitting or crocheting with it. But many artisanal yarns are sold in what are called "hanks" or "skeins," which need to be wound before you work with them, or else you will end up with a tangled mess.

Winding these skeins takes a bit of time, and sometimes a lot of patience. The right equipment makes it easier, but that equipment is a bit pricey. So, many yarn stores either charge for the service, or refuse to wind the yarn altogether. Other stores will wind your yarn, but only if you bought it in their store. (Some store owners have gotten famously incensed for being asked to wind yarn that's been purchased elsewhere.)

But my thinking was, if they've walked through my door, I'm gonna do whatever I can to help them be successful. My mantra? "Yarn should be the happiest part of your day."

So we had two swift-and-winder apparatuses set up, and we would wind yarn from anywhere, even if it came from Queen Bee's store. (Okay, *especially* from Queen Bee's store.)

The third big difference about the Loops store layout was that we had a huge playroom, filled with a Thomas the train table, a TV with a VHS player, a collection of some of my kids' favorite movies, and tons of toys and imaginative play settings to spark creativity.

The purpose of the playroom was twofold: One, so my own kids could stay entertained while Mommy was working late. And two, so every parent and grandparent who ever came into Loops would know that children were not only allowed but encouraged.

Word began to spread.

Each day, the bell on the front door rang more and more often.

My "Loops blue" ocean strategy was working.

CHAPTER 11

THE FABRIC

I'm telling you, there is nothing more rewarding than when another human being shares with you that your business—you, your product, your team, and the environment you've created—have helped save their life.

From the earliest days of Loops, I witnessed the healing power of knitting. From the start, we had lots of customers who were going through chemo—since Utica Square was right across the street from a major medical center. So many of these sweet patients would come in, frustrated and in tears by the unexpected effect they referred to as "chemo brain." Even though they had entered treatment with positivity and determination, planning to use the time to catch up on reading or some other cerebral activity, they now found themselves "foggy" and unable to concentrate.

We would gently guide these customers to simple, meditative knitting patterns and soft, soft yarn in beautiful colors—you could see the texture and hues instantly lift their spirits. And they would come back, a few days later, all lit up with joy. The knitting process calmed them, soothed their spirits, and helped them transform their feeling of helplessness into a powerful, quiet productivity. The gratitude of these patients was a palpable gift, and we all celebrated together when they "rang the bell" on their last chemo treatments.

And here's something most yarn people already know: There is a magic that happens on the sofa of a yarn store that's unlike anything else I've ever seen.

Knitters and crocheters of all ages, races, religions, abilities, and backgrounds come together there. With yarn gliding through their fingers and the steady *click-click-click* of needles and hooks, an unseen bond, a palpable glow seems to rise and emanate from the group. In this safe container of creativity, the usual defenses dissolve, and the words begin to flow.

Supported by the shared love of fiber, real conversation happens. Real connections happen. A fabric forms. Something from practically nothing: Just sticks and string.

When I think about these "couch connections," I often think about my friend Angie.

In the early days of Loops, Angie was going through a really tough divorce under especially difficult circumstances. She and her soon-to-be ex had one child, a pre-teen daughter who was especially sweet and sensitive. Angie confided in me that she was having trouble talking to her daughter. Every time she tried to open a conversation, especially about the divorce, her daughter just clammed up.

Then Angie had an idea. One day, she casually suggested to her daughter that they sit down and knit together. Angie would teach her. And as soon as her daughter got the basics down, and they settled into a quiet knitting rhythm together . . . then, *magic*. The spout opened and all of the daughter's emotions—anger, frustration, fear, tears—came pouring out. It was the beginning of a healing journey for both of them.

Angie's story showed me that creativity—in almost any form—has the potential to become a form of ministry. When people come together through a creative commonality, even something as seemingly simple as knitting, a profound connection can form. And in the safe space that's created, it becomes possible to have the more difficult, more meaningful, more important conversations.

If only the Loops couch could talk! It's held space for so many respectful and even transformative conversations around really tough topics like race, religion, LGBTQ rights, reproductive rights, gun laws, and end-of-life issues. These couch conversations can lead directly to true understanding and lasting, positive change. When you start with a common bond, some sticks and strings and conversation, it's amazing the fabric that you can create together.

WHAT TO REMEMBER AS YOU MOVE AHEAD . . .

Creativity is the new currency. Never apologize for your creative power. Believe in it. Nurture it. Own it! If you can find a way to turn your hobby into your jobby, you're one giant step closer to living your dream. Work becomes play, meetings morph into playdates, and even the toughest challenges turn into adrenaline-filled obstacle courses. Yes, you may work harder than you ever imagined you could. But it will always feel a little like you're getting away with something—in the best possible way.

Lean into your creativity with every step. When you catch yourself feeling "less than" because you don't have an M.B.A., or lack the tech training, or accounting skills, or whatever . . . remember your secret weapon: tap into your creativity. Knit the cashmere scarf that gets you the lease deal. Craft and cobble together the product or service the world has been waiting for. Swim for the blue ocean and leave the sharks to fight it out in the red water you left behind.

Burst bubbles are a gift. When your idea gets rejected the first time, or someone gives you feedback that stings a little at first, remember you still have a thousand other ideas in your head. Unlike profit margins and balance sheets, your creativity is not finite. Lick your wounds for a minute if you must, but get back on that tricycle as soon as you can and start looking for the next idea. It's bound to be better than the last. And when you're down the road a bit and able to look back with perspective, you'll see exactly how the dots connected to form the perfect path.

There's magic in shared creation. It's never really just sticks and string. When you bring people together through the shared joy of creation, really cool things start to happen. Conversations spark. Healing begins. Your Big Why begins to emerge. And once you've glimpsed a vision of where your creativity can take you, well, there's really no stopping you now.

Your Second Move

JUST KEEP
MOVING

CHAPTER 12

YOU MAY NOT BE PERFECT

The first piece of framed art I remember owning was an illustration of a freckle-faced girl, accompanied by a charming handwritten phrase: "I may not be perfect, but parts of me are excellent."

My mother gave it to me.

It was cute. And I remember that, when she gave it to me, her mood was serious, intentional. Like this was a phrase I should really take in, ingest as part of my being on the journey to adulthood. But something about it never sat right with me.

Why *can't* I be perfect?

Shouldn't all mothers believe their child is perfect?

What was wrong with me?

Many years later, in my early 30s, I confessed to my mother how this picture, hanging on the wall of my childhood bedroom, had always bothered me. That, growing up, I saw my mother as perfect. And that when she hung this on my wall, I took it to mean I could never be as good as her.

Rather than sensing the vulnerability of the moment, my mom seemed annoyed. She said I should be happy that I had turned out so well . . . and hadn't she done a great job? She just wasn't getting what I was saying: that the gap between my perception of her as perfect, and the picture's assertion that I was not, made me feel I would forever be "less than."

Then, the following Christmas, my mom presented me with a wrapped gift. She could barely contain her excitement as I started to open it. I think I audibly gasped when I unwrapped a large, framed needlepoint creation with flowers and old-English letters that read: "I may not be perfect, but parts of me are excellent." Had she not heard me say how much that sentiment had hurt and confused me all of these years?

But apparently, Mom took my gasp to mean I was shocked at all the effort she'd put into making it. "I've been working on it for months!" Mom beamed.

It took me a couple more decades, a fair amount of therapy, and a whole lot of failure to realize that perfection is neither attainable nor, in the end, desirable.

In fact, perfection is the enemy of progress.

Knitters learn this very quickly. While we may aspire to perfection as we create our first scarf or first sweater . . . over the course of the thousands of stitches that will make up that sweater, it's inevitable—you're going to make a mistake. Even if you fix that mistake, there will be another, and yet another. And even if you made every stitch perfectly, your tension would vary ever so slightly, with some stitches being more stretched than others, based on the level of stress in your life that day, or the lighting of the room you were in, or the temperature, or the weather. As you complete project after project, you learn to accept and even embrace the inconsistencies in each knitted garment, and you even take pride in the learned ability to resolve complex mistakes and move forward.

It took me longer to learn the same lesson as an entrepreneur, but the lesson was even more valuable.

My friend Susan Garrett, who is a multiple-time World Champion in the sport of dog agility, likes to say, "There is no losing. Every time I step into the ring, I either win, or I learn."

When you step into the ring of entrepreneurship, it is inevitable. You are going to stretch far beyond your comfort zone, and in doing so, you are going to fail. What's not inevitable is how you choose to react.

The faster you can learn to accept those failures as opportunities to optimize, the faster you will achieve your goals.

So, from the very start, set aside the illusion of perfectionism. Set yourself on a course to fail forward. Resolve that—*no matter what*—you will just keep moving and learning and growing.

CHAPTER 13

THE
DIAGNOSIS

Eighteen months after Brent and I were married, our first child, Sam, was born.

It had been a challenging pregnancy. I had 24/7 nausea for the first four months, and the only thing that gave me relief was eating. I gave up running, because it made me nauseous too. I tried water aerobics, but the smell of chlorine made me even sicker.

Without the endorphins from exercise, and with my surging hormones, my anxiety went through the roof. I gained sixty pounds.

The delivery was unusually challenging too. I was about a week past due, and they thought the baby was large, so they scheduled an inducement. That very morning, I woke to a popping sound—and sure enough, my water broke! Yet, things still moved along slowly, and it took more than 24 hours for Samuel William Brander to make his entrance into the world.

And what an entrance he made!

Every half hour, when the nurses would bring Sam to me, he would always be crying hysterically. He had a strangely sweet cry and we soon dubbed him "the Sammy lamby" because he sounded like a bleating lamb. As soon as he finished nursing, the nurses would take him back to the nursery. I would just start to drift off . . . and here they'd come again, wheeling Sam in his bassinet.

"But I just fed him," I would protest, exhausted.

"We know, but he won't stop crying. Are you sure he's getting enough milk?" they asked, over and over and over.

The lactation consultant came and confirmed that yes, I was producing plenty, and Sam was getting plenty. "He must just be hungry after all of that work, coming into the world!" they joked.

I wasn't laughing.

Brent hanging out with Sam, our first-born.

Then it came time to leave the hospital and go home. Brent and I both remember, vividly, the moment when we were standing at the sliding doors, trying to put Sam into his car seat. He wouldn't stop screaming. We looked at each other, my husband and I, and thought the exact same thought: We Are Not Ready For This.

Little did we know exactly how Not Ready we were.

We got Sam home, but the screaming continued. We would walk around the house, rocking and cuddling him while he cried. He wanted to nurse constantly. The only time he would sleep was right after he finished nursing, and only for a few minutes. This went on for 48 hours. We were all zombies.

After the fifth frantic call to the pediatrician after-hours line, we were told to head straight to the E.R.

They took one look at Sam's tomato-red face and put us right into a triage room. In walked the doctor, all business. He gave us a quick once-over glance and you could see him arrive instantly at his "diagnosis": Overprotective, exhausted parents.

But Sam had another plan. He was going to get this doctor's attention.

As the doctor asked us a series of routine, robotic questions, Sam continued to scream and scream and scream. The doctor seemed unphased and uninterested as he unwrapped Sam's diaper, asking, "Has he urinated today?" at the exact moment that Sam let loose a big, healthy urine stream—right in the doctor's face.

"Well, I guess that answers that question," he said grimly.

A second doctor with a better bedside manner decided that Sam simply had a severe case of colic. He gave us all kinds of tips: Try raising the head of the crib. Try Mylicon drops. Try long walks. And if all else fails, put Sam in the crib, put in your earplugs, and let him cry while you sleep.

None of it helped.

For six weeks—42 days—our sweet little Sam never slept more than one hour at a time. We walked him in the stroller, all over the neighborhood—and walked and walked and walked. When the cry would return, we took to the car. We drove and drove and drove. Sam seemed to love the drives, the hum of the highway, the twists and the turns. Sometimes he would sleep, but more often, Brent and I would glance back and see that his blue eyes were wide open, taking in the passing landscapes. And then we would get home, and the cry would return.

All of my carefully laid plans—to place Sam in the perfect day-care and return to full-time work at the shiny new office space we had just leased for Branders, Inc.—all flew right out the window. My child was miserable. Nothing else mattered.

I was so exhausted and numb, I don't even remember moving my files and office furniture home, turning the tiny living room of our two-bedroom house into a makeshift workspace. In my severely sleep-deprived state, writing was nearly impossible. We were going back and forth to the pediatrician's office several times a week, desperately seeking any sort of solution.

Then late one night (or rather, early one morning), after Sam and I had just finished another in our seemingly endless carousel of nursing sessions, I logged onto a website called Moms Online. This was at the advent of online forums, when everyone still had an AOL address. This website had become something of a lifeline for me—hanging out in the middle of the night with other clueless new moms at the end of their own ropes.

And there, in a nursing thread, was a simple suggestion that no one—my pediatrician, my family, my well-meaning friends—had thought to offer.

"Try taking dairy out of your own diet," someone had suggested to another mom of a colicky baby.

Somewhere in the dim recesses of my insomnia-addled brain, I remembered hearing that, as an infant, I'd had to be on soy formula, which was very rare at that time. And something stirred within me: the faint flicker of hope. I decided then and there to go dairy-free.

The next night, after less than 24 hours of a dairy-free diet, Sam slept through the night.

And we slept like the dead. It was the most blissful possible experience, waking up that next morning after our first REM sleep in a month and a half.

From that point through his first year of life, Sam developed normally. He was still a little fussy in the evenings, but it was barely noticeable compared with his first six weeks. He was a busy little boy who always wanted to be on the go. He hit all of his physical milestones really early—rolling over, sitting up, crawling, walking, and running way ahead of what had been predicted in my trusty *What to Expect* books.

He especially loved working on puzzles, and he was particularly attached to two of them—one with the letters of the alphabet, and the other a map of the United States.

Another funny thing: When we took Sam for drives, he seemed to have an uncanny sense of direction. We'd say, "We're going to Nonna's house," but if we went a slightly different route—for instance, detouring to get gas—Sam would get agitated. From his backward-facing car seat, he would point in the direction we normally went to Nonna's, and make urgent little sounds, trying to get us back on the "right" route.

While Sam was super-engaging with adults and older kids—he loved being the life of the party—things were different with babies his own age. For his first preschool experience we dropped him off at a mother's day out, and he clung desperately to my leg, crying. Nothing unusual about that, I thought. What was unusual was when we picked him up, several hours later, he was still crying in a corner, separated from all the other kids. The teacher reported that he'd been like that all morning.

"Huh," we thought. "That's not like the Sam we know."

Then, at about 12 months, Sam began to lose the few words he'd acquired. We weren't too concerned at first. Then we realized he'd also stopped doing most of his barnyard animal impressions, when previously he'd loved to regale a roomful of adults with his "doggie" and "horsey" and "cow."

My mommy alarm bell started going off. Quietly at first, in the distant recesses of my mind. And then louder and louder, until I admitted to myself that it was time to act.

We took Sam to a developmental specialist. She ran him through the full battery of tests, and to our great relief, pronounced him completely normal. She said it was typical for language to ebb and flow in the beginning. We should just keep an eye on it but try not to obsess over it.

"Not obsessing" was not going to be easy, especially because at this point, my hormones were surging again—because I was five months pregnant with our first little girl.

My second pregnancy was a roller coaster from start to finish. The lows began when I woke in the night to nurse Sam (who was then nine months old) and passed out cold on my bedroom floor. The strain of my body nursing *and* being pregnant was taking its toll. There was no nutrition left for me! I'd lost all 60 pounds of my baby weight from Sam, and then some.

Then came the nausea—again. And back came the 60 pounds—again! It seemed my body was designed for giant baby weight gain, along with giant babies. I blamed my 6'6" father and 5'2" mother for confusing the gene pool. My body was tricked into thinking I could deliver huge babies.

When Cecily Holland was born in August 1997, she weighed in at 10 pounds, 8 ounces. They had scheduled my inducement two weeks early—so if she had gone to full term, she would have been more than 12 pounds! She came into the world looking like a six-month-old infant. And from the start, she was the opposite of Sam when it came to temperament. I had to call the nurses to remind them to bring her to me to eat. She would snuggle up into my arms, just content to be with me, not demanding anything. She was all gentleness, quietness, calmness. It was a balm to my jangled mommy nerves.

Sam was instantly attached to his new baby sister. He loved bringing her a blanket, a pacifier, or even his own toys to "play" with, and often we would find him just staring adoringly at her. There was just one little issue: Whenever Cecily would cry (which was exceedingly rare), Sam would walk over and give her a little shove.

When we asked Sam why he did it, he just said, "Stop." By this point, I'd gotten pretty good at interpreting Sam-ese, so I understood that he just wanted to make Cecily stop crying.

We were constantly on edge, worrying that Cecily might wake up and cry, and Sam would try to "stop" it. We had to keep a nonstop eye on both of them. So, back we went to the child development specialist. She ran another round of tests. And this time, she had a different result to share.

"I think Sam may be on the autistic spectrum."

The WHAT?!

And thus began the phase of my life I now refer to as "manic mommy phase."

Keep in mind, this was 1997. Long before it was fashionable to have an autistic character in every TV series, book, and movie. At this point in time, my full understanding of autism could be summed up in two words: *Rain Man*. That was the 1988 Oscar-winning movie starring Dustin Hoffman and Tom Cruise, where Hoffman plays an autistic man confined to a mental institution.

This was *not* my child. They *must* be wrong.

I jumped into action.

My first step was to call the developmental pediatrician who was widely known to be the self-proclaimed autism expert for Tulsa. Sam was placed on the doctor's waitlist, and I was told to expect at least an eight-month wait.

No way was I going to sit around for eight months.

So next, I ordered the top-rated book on autism (back then, there were only a handful on the market; today there are 75 *pages* worth of listings on Amazon). The first book I read, *Let Me Hear Your Voice* by Catherine Maurice, stressed the importance of treatment before the "neurological window closes, around the age of five."

Full-on panic set in.

Followed shortly thereafter by full-on, unstoppable-locomotive-mom determination. The clock was ticking.

I read every book I could get my hands on. Then I started digging into websites, drilling down into medical journals, research findings, obscure cases, and possible cures. I called around, assembling a treatment team. The most promising treatment seemed to be something called Applied Behavior Analysis—ABA, for short. Very few people in Tulsa were familiar with it, but if I found someone who knew what ABA was, and I got a good feeling from them, they were hired.

Before long, my 18-month-old kiddo had a Ph.D. psychiatrist (who knew about ABA through her own research, because her own son was autistic), three college-aged speech therapy students, an occupational therapist, and a sensory integration therapist. We quickly worked up a schedule that gave Sam 40 hours a week in therapy. Insurance wouldn't cover anything. It was going to cost a fortune. I didn't care. I just worked harder, writing more ads, and spending all night researching possible treatments.

I started to notice a lot of "fringe" research around diet treatments for autism. In particular, a lot of kids on the spectrum seemed to be responding well to diets free of casein (milk protein) and something called "gluten." I'd never heard of either, but I knew from hard-earned experience that Sam and dairy were not friends. I decided to give this casein-free, gluten-free thing a try.

Every single member of our family thought we were crazy. Who ever heard of a child deprived of pizza, chicken nuggets, even basic bread, for God's sake? It became the main topic of conversation at family gatherings. We would see our family members exchanging looks, even rolling their eyes.

Eventually, we started showing up at family events carrying Sam's meals in discreet brown paper bags. Still, we couldn't miss the sideways glances of confusion and worse, pity. But we believed we were seeing some improvement in Sam, and we weren't about to jeopardize that. One time, at a cousin's birthday party, a well-meaning uncle snuck a piece of birthday cake to Sam, and the results were immediate—bright red face rash followed shortly by stomach cramps and diarrhea. This further strengthened our resolve. Something was going on with Sam and these substances.

To help shore up our stance that diet was somehow connected to Sam's condition, we took him to a traditional allergist, who confirmed that Sam was allergic to pretty much everything—wheat, dairy, soy, eggs, nuts, chocolate. The doctor recommended the "caveman diet" of simply meat, fresh veggies, and fruit. We were lucky that Sam wasn't a picky eater, like so many kids on the spectrum. He happily ate almost anything we put in front of him! But it was sad that, at preschool, Sam couldn't eat all the Cheez-Its and goldfish and Teddy Grahams that were standard toddler fare. It just served to separate him even further from his peers.

Then one day, Sam had another loose stool—but this time, he hadn't had any of the off-limits foods.

And it got worse. Much worse. Sam quickly became so ill, he couldn't get off the couch, couldn't even sit up. He was ghostly pale and listless.

We rushed in to see the pediatrician, who did all the usual tests, all with negative results. The doctor was stumped. He decided to run a series of a dozen or so more tests, and told us to go home, try to keep Sam hydrated, and wait for the results. As we were headed out the door, I turned and asked, "Hey, I read online about something called C. Diff? Remember, Sam was on antibiotics for an ear infection last month. Any chance it could be that?"

Our pediatrician, who I'd carefully selected for his kindness and open-mindedness, shook his head. "Almost every C. Diff diagnosis is in the elderly population," he said. Then, seeing the pleading look on my face, he said, "Well, I guess it won't hurt to add the test to the list."

After a long and harrowing night with Sam, the doctor called, at last. "You're not going to believe this, but you were right!" he said. "It's C Diff." When I asked him what the treatment was, he said, "I know this sounds odd, but the treatment is another antibiotic, a much stronger one."

We started Sam on the new antibiotic, and within an hour, I knew something was very, very wrong. Sam became more listless than ever. His skin was now gray. With rising panic, I looked up C. Diff and cross-referenced with the prescribed antibiotic. Instantly, articles popped up about the dangers of this drug, and that it had been shown to be counterproductive, even deadly, especially for small children with C. Diff. I dug deeper, increasingly desperate to find an alternative. I ran across a tiny, "fringe" article about a promising probiotic called Culturelle, that could only be ordered directly from the manufacturer. PRObiotic, in that moment, made so much more sense to me than another

ANTIbiotic. I called the company, reached a human, and convinced them to overnight it to me.

That night, Sam slept next to me, breathing raggedly, as I prayed and watched the clock, every minute ticking by, agonizingly slowly. I held my breath all night, and finally fell asleep around 4 A.M.

At 6 A.M. I awoke to Sam jumping out of bed and declaring, "I feel good, Mommy!"

From this point on, it was All Systems Go when it came to nutritional and alternative therapies.

Tests showed that Sam's body was not good at processing metals, and that he had the maximum possible concentration of antimony in his bloodstream. At the time, antimony was often used as a fire-retardant on things like cribs and baby pajamas, and Sam had a habit of teething on his crib rail and chewing on the neck of his pajamas.

He also had evidence of yeast overgrowth and "leaky gut syndrome." I did lots of research on food allergies and came to understand that these conditions can occur in susceptible children as a result of diet as well as overuse of antibiotics. Food does not get properly broken down, and can impair brain function, the articles said.

Suddenly, everything started to make sense: Sam's miserable first six weeks of life, before I removed dairy from my breastfeeding diet; Sam's negative reaction to three major classes of antibiotics in his first year of life; the loss of some speech after his 12-month immunizations, which at that time still ALL contained mercury (Thimerosal—which has since been removed); Sam's steady improvement on a casein - and gluten-free diet; and the incredible rebound from his deathbed with a single dose of strong probiotics.

At our next appointment with Dr. H (the Ph.D. psychologist leading Sam's treatment team), I told her the latest, dramatic development with Sam's nutritional therapies. We had decided to start Sam on an antifungal treatment for the yeast overgrowth. The very next day, we saw two dramatic shifts. It was so black-and-white that we were astonished.

First, when Sam woke up that morning, he said, "I want some juice, please." At first I didn't even register what a huge deal this was. Then I remembered: From the time he started speaking, Sam had been echolalic, a common marker in autistic children. They get their pronouns reversed, and echo what they've always heard. So an autistic child will echo what they've always heard Mom or Dad say, such as: "You want some juice?" When they really mean, "I want some juice." A neurotypical child is able to naturally flip it and use the correct pronoun. So when Sam used the correct "I" for the first time ever in this situation . . . and the magnitude of it hit me . . . my jaw dropped.

Second, when we headed to Sam's favorite playground (where I'd promised to take him that morning), we witnessed a miracle.

Sam loved running, climbing, jumping, and climbing some more, but he always did it alone. If there were other kids on the playground, he kept a safe distance and never engaged. But on *this* day, the day after he started the antifungal treatment, to my disbelief he ran onto the playground, right up to another kid he'd never met. "You wanna play with me?" he said. And they immediately paired up, ran around and played together for an hour. Over on the bench, this stunned mom sat smiling, tears streaming down my face.

As I related all of this to Dr. H, I watched her expression go from her usual calm, dispassionate "doctor face," to surprise, shock, and something I hadn't seen there before . . .

hope. Hope not only for Sam, but for her own son, who was older and more severely affected by the disorder.

She told me that, when I had first mentioned the diet and alternative therapies, she had inwardly dismissed them. "But I didn't want to take away your hope, and they all sounded reasonably safe, so what could it hurt?" We talked through any other factors that might have been at play. Was there anything different or unusual in Sam's PT and OT treatments? Anything new at school, at home, in any other environment?

Nothing else made sense. And, seeing the undeniable results in Sam, Dr. H had to admit she was convinced.

I've since lost touch with Dr. H, but the last time we chatted, her son had begun to have great success with many of the same treatments that worked for Sam. And today, of course, "gluten-free" and "dairy-free" are all the rage, with aisle after aisle of convenience products at Whole Foods. It's become almost automatic for newly diagnosed children on the spectrum to go on this diet, and the gut (biome) connection to spectrum disorders is being increasingly studied in the scientific community.

By the time Sam reached the age of five—that crucial milestone in the first book I read by Catherine Maurice—his therapists declared him to be "recovered" from autism.

I know this is a controversial statement to make. And has Sam still struggled? Sure. School has always been a challenge for him, especially the transitions like grade school to middle school and high school to college. But the "bigger pond" of college turned out to be much better for Sam. He joined a fraternity, and openly shared (for the first time) with his new brothers about the struggles he'd been through. They embraced him, even vowing to help him overcome his shyness with girls—something he's still working on! And Sam was thrilled to find that Oklahoma State University offered a degree in his first love—geography. He soaked up his geography courses, earned almost all As throughout college, and even had a short study abroad experience in Cambridge, England, before graduating.

Sam Brander, graduate with honors, Oklahoma State University.

As of this writing, Sam is working full-time as a geospatial analyst in Tulsa and looking forward to his first apartment and his first girlfriend. He loves riding his road bike, working out at the gym, raking leaves, volunteer work, and most of all, traveling. He still loves road trips and maps, and still connects best with people who are older or younger than him—peer relationships can be awkward. Luckily, as we've always told him . . . the older you get, the less anyone knows your age, so the less that matters!

The fight to save Sam—and looking back, that's absolutely what it was, a fight—had a profound impact on me, not just as a mom, but as an entrepreneur, and more fundamentally, as a human being. From what seemed at the time to be the ultimate parent's nightmare, came a beautiful gift. The trauma helped me find a deep, deep well of energy and resourcefulness and fearlessness that I never knew I had.

Not a day seems to go by without someone asking me, "Do you ever sleep? How do you find time to run a business/ raise a family/knit a sweater/write a book?"

I just smile and tell them yes, I sleep—although not always as well as I'd like.

And then I assure them: I'm human. I did what any mom would do when the stakes are this high. You too have so much more energy than you know. Trust that it will be there for you when you need it most.

CHAPTER 14

YOU CAN'T MAKE A LIVING WITH YARN

Every entrepreneur has the same well of energy and optimism that pushed me into action after Sam's diagnosis. I had no way of knowing how often I'd need to return to that well—how deep I'd have to dig—on the long Loops journey that lay ahead. I just knew I had a big idea, and I had to keep moving forward.

The day of the Queen Bee incident, I came home and announced my intention to Brent: "I'm going to open a yarn store."

"Ummmm . . . what?" he said.

I told him what I'd just experienced. Told him there had to be a better way. Confessed that I'd been building a vision of a new business in my head for a while, a more modern take on the yarn store. In my store, everything would be super-organized, so busy people could run in, grab a great project, and go. In my store, everyone would be super-friendly, ready to help. In my store, all knitters and crocheters, of all ages, would be welcome. My store would be a community where people from all walks of life could come together and share their life experiences, united by their common love of yarn.

Brent broke into my reverie: "So how are you going to do all this and Branders, Inc., too?"

"I'll figure it out."

"Well . . . okay. It's pretty crazy. But if anyone can do it, you can," he said.

That very night, I called my friend Scott, the only person I could think of with an MBA.

"Will you help me write a business plan?" I asked him.

"What for?" he said. "Isn't your business already going great?"

"Let's meet and I'll explain," I said.

I had a couple of days before my lunch with Scott, so I started doing some research. I found reports from the Craft Yarn Council of America and The National Needlework Association. It wasn't terribly encouraging. The average yarn store reported total sales of less than $100,000 per year. Take half off the top for inventory, more for rent and keeping the lights on . . . and it didn't take a master's degree to see that this was just a hobby for most people. A very expensive hobby.

So next, I called Sylvia, my mom's friend from North Carolina who'd taught me to knit at 16, almost two decades earlier. At that point, Sylvia had sold her yarn shop and become a traveling yarn rep. I explained my plan to her.

"OH! You should totally do it!" she said. "You'll be great at it, and you'll have so much fun!" Then I asked her how long it might take before I could leave the branding business and support our family with the yarn store.

"Oh, honey . . . I really hate to tell you this, and I don't wanna crush your dream," she said. "But you need to know: you can't make a living with yarn."

So by the time I sat down for sushi with Scott, I was feeling a bit more apprehensive. I remember it was my first time being served edamame. My nerves were already so jangly that this unfamiliar food just made me more anxious. But Scott was politely waiting for me to go first, so I hesitantly picked up a pod. Not knowing I was supposed to squeeze out the edamame "seeds," I bit into the pod and chewed it instead! Why in the world did people like this stuff so much?!

To his credit, Scott just watched with a bemused smile, and then plucked a pod, squeezed out the edible bits, ate them, and placed the empty pod in the extra bowl supplied for this purpose. Oh Lordy, I was so embarrassed. But I had already learned something. Eating edamame the right way was delicious! So I decided it was time to plunge ahead with the business at hand.

I showed him all my research and shared the bones of my business plan, which I'd put together from a template I'd found online. The document detailed my long-range goal to franchise Loops. I also shared the conversation I'd had with Sylvia, including her dire warning.

Scott looked through it all, scribbled a few numbers, and said he'd take it home and work on it. Then he looked me square in the eye.

"I'm not going to sugarcoat it. It's going to be tough. You need to be prepared to *not* take a dollar from it for at least the first three years. You're going to work your ass off."

I let this sink in for a moment. Something deep inside locked itself into place. I could practically hear the padlock. No matter how long it took, no matter how hard I had to juggle both businesses and my growing family, Loops was going to be a success story.

"But I'm with Brent: if anyone can do this, you can," Scott was saying. Then he added with a wink, "Just get ready, 'cause someday, everyone's gonna call you Loops Lady."

CHAPTER 15

IF THEY CAN DO IT, I CAN DO IT

You know how you can want something so much, for so long, and then when you finally get it, you're like . . . OH SH*T. What now?

Well, now it was time to open a yarn store. And despite my fancy business plan, despite my grand ideas and hopes and dreams, the reality was that I had no idea what I was doing.

I'd never managed inventory—unless you counted pricing thousands of Christmas ornaments in a sweltering summer warehouse during one of my high school jobs.

I'd never managed sales—unless you counted selling Camp Fire candy, or my various waitressing jobs in college.

And most of all, I'd never managed people—unless you counted my sister, who worked as the office manager for Branders, Inc.—and that particular employer-employee relationship was about to end. Badly.

My only sibling is five years younger than me. Brilliant, kind, and gifted at organization, she had been the sole employee of Branders, Inc. for several years. She called herself the "office nannager" because, in addition to helping manage the office, she helped out as a nanny to our three kids.

She has a math degree and a beautiful mind for systems and organization. This provided a great balance to my act-now-ask-questions-later entrepreneurial work style. And she was fantastic with the kids, who all adored her. On the surface, it seemed like the perfect situation.

But of course, things are rarely as they seem on the surface.

The deep, dark reality was that, at this point in time, Brent and I were really struggling to keep our heads above water. At the very moment that we discovered we'd be building and opening a new retail store, Branders, Inc. was crushing it. One of our biggest clients, the Cherokee Nation, had partnered with Hard Rock Casinos to re-brand its primary property. Our personal work schedule had started to resemble that of a gambling addict. We worked so many hours, we didn't know if it was day or night! Our bank account was flourishing, but our stress levels were through the roof.

For my sister, that meant increased workload, increased stress, *and* the added bonus of taking care of three kids who were often very unhappy that Mommy and Daddy were always "still working" and couldn't come out to play.

The breaking point came the day that I told my sister about the news from Utica Square. "We're going to open Loops in May, and my goal is to be out of the branding business within a year."

I'll never forget how she looked at me.

Like I'd just sprouted six more heads.

"Okay, that's it. You're officially out of your mind," she said. "I am *so done.*"

I was genuinely shocked by her words. I'd been sure she would be elated. Maybe I'd misunderstood her?

"I mean sure, it'll be a lot of work," I said. "But it's really exciting! It'll be a new adventure for us all! Right?"

Her response? "I can't believe you would risk your whole FAMILY. Brent, the kids, me. I can't believe you would throw all of this away on this crazy idea!"

And it only escalated from there. It ended with harsh words—all that frustration from years of pent-up stress all around—and my sister walked out. It turned out to be the right move, for both of us, as she was able to move on to building her own career, moving beyond her big sister's shadow, and today our relationship is the best it's ever been. But back then, it felt like a complete disaster. It meant that Brent and I now had three kids under five, a booming branding business that I desperately wanted out of, a retail store to open from scratch, and no employees, no childcare, no support.

Good times.

In my darker, most anxious moments, I would ask myself, *WHAT are you doing? A retail store? Everyone knows the statistics—you're pretty much doomed to fail. Your sister is right. Why are you putting your family at risk? Why take the chance?*

And then I would go for a drive.

I would drive past strip centers filled with tiny businesses.

I would drive past huge retail superstores.

I would drive past office buildings, new car lots, used car lots, pizza joints. Hundreds and hundreds of businesses in this one city I called home.

Every one of those businesses has an owner, and every business started with a dream, I told myself.

And I tapped back into that padlocked resolve, felt it growing even stronger.

"If they can do it, I can do it."

CHAPTER 16

THE WALL

In the early 2000s, yarn was booming, the height of what the National Needlearts Association referred to as an ongoing 10-year retail cycle. New yarn stores were popping up, rapid-fire, all over North America. The best yarn reps stalked the fertile waters like sharks, looking for the prize fish—which, unbeknownst to me, was the naïve new shop owner.

The lucky shark who was first to the fish could stock the pond full of all his lines. (And yes, I use the pronoun "he" because most of the reps were men.) This was key because, at this time, there was tremendous overlap in inventory from one yarn company to the next. Most of the yarn originated from the same places, Italy and Germany, and a lot of it was basically the same exact fiber, sold under different labels.

Each yarn rep knew, if he could get to a new store owner *first*, he could educate her on the range of fibers she would need. She would knit her store models with his yarns, and then she would need to re-order those same yarns over and over, for years to come. In the process, he would build trust with the owner, as she would come to rely on his expertise. And this would, in effect, build a 20-foot wall between him and his competition.

The first yarn rep to schedule a meeting with me and Emma was named Dave. When we scheduled the meeting, Dave said to plan for two hours. The meeting went eight hours *the first day,* and we still weren't done. Dave left, checked into a hotel, promising to be back at eight the next morning.

As the meeting finally wound to a close, Dave told me he had rescheduled a planned trip to another state, just so he could meet with me.

Puzzled, I asked him why.

"It was that Wall idea," Dave said.

When Dave and I had first spoken over the phone, I'd told him my idea for what I called the Hot Loops Wall. It was inspired by my earliest yarn shopping experiences, when I'd spent countless hours in stores and left, empty-handed, because I couldn't find anything I really wanted to make. Yarn stores were such mazes to me.

"So my idea is to create a wall made up of a series of columns. At the top will be the photo of a finished project, then the next shelf down will have the pattern, and then the next shelves down will have the yarn, all curated and arranged nice and neat. So a busy knitter can run into the store, grab a great project, and get out the door fast. Less time shopping, more time knitting!" I exclaimed.

Dave told me why this idea had caught his attention and made him alter his schedule to come see me.

"It wasn't the idea itself. In fact, I'm betting you'll get tired of that Wall and it'll be gone in a couple years. But it was the fact you had an original idea to begin with. Most people who start yarn stores have no plan at all."

He continued: "I've been doing this for decades now, and I see it over and over. Most times someone takes up the hobby, falls in love with the yarn, and thinks it would be fun to have their own store full of yarn. Simple as that. No business plan. No backup plan. It breaks my heart to see them open and close, open and close. But I could tell, you were different. I think you're gonna make it."

I didn't really register that last part. I was still stuck back on Dave saying the Hot Loops Wall wouldn't last more than two years.

This year, Loops celebrated 15 years in business, with 30 new Hot Loops Walls under our belts.

It's become one of our most iconic features.

The Hot Loops Wall™ helps customers "find a great project, fast."

Each trademarked Hot Loops Wall is indeed a big undertaking that today requires the full effort of our entire team—researching trends and patterns, working with dyers to create exclusive colorways, knitting and crocheting all the projects, photographing the finished pieces, putting it all together.

And each season, as a new Wall comes together, I think of Dave (who, over the years, became one of my most trusted advisors until his well-deserved retirement).

Dave helped me see the value of a creative plan—any plan—but especially one that sets you apart from your competitors. And by issuing his unintended challenge that the Wall wouldn't endure, Dave helped me see the value of *sticking to that plan.*

Especially when you're just starting out, it's so tempting to pivot too soon. It's easy to second-guess yourself. But I think, in the early days, you should set a plan—any plan—and stick with it, until all the evidence and, most of all, your gut tells you otherwise. Believe in your original ideas, and in the immortal words of Dory the Fish from the movie *Finding Nemo*, "Just keep swimming."

CHAPTER 17

IS THIS A GOOD DEAL FOR YOU?

By the end of that two-day meeting with my first yarn rep, I'd spent 80 percent of the budget I'd allocated for the entire store's inventory. (Nicely played, Dave!) And within just a few days, the boxes started arriving.

Almost instantly, our home's entire glassed-in porch was stacked to the ceiling with big brown boxes of yarn. The porch had been the kids' playroom, so they retreated to their bedrooms, where Brent would watch over them, as Emma and I began the task of labeling thousands and thousands of balls of yarn. At first, each day was like the ultimate Christmas morning, with Emma and I wielding our box cutters, tearing into each box, and plucking a fresh, plastic-wrapped bag of colorful fiber from inside and thrusting it into the air victoriously. "Ahhhh, look at this one! So pretty!" "Oooh, see this one? I can't wait to make something with this!"

But very quickly, we understood how easy it was to accidentally slide the box cutter blade through to the contents inside, and inadvertently ruin 30 balls of yarn at once. We learned to slow down, to very carefully insert the box knife just below the surface of the box, so as not to damage its cargo. We also were shocked to learn how poorly most yarn companies packaged their goods. Many of them obviously reused their boxes and, while we appreciated the attempt at environmental responsibility, we were dismayed when re-used and dilapidated diaper boxes and liquor boxes arrived, often with gaping holes and yarn spilling out.

I would sometimes take photos of these boxes and send them to the yarn companies, encouraging them to upgrade their box choices and preserve their merchandise. This was one of the early indicators to me that, in so many ways, the yarn industry was years—or even decades—behind the rest of the developed world when it came to sales and commerce.

Another indicator of that was the antiquated sales rep system. I felt like I had gone back in time to the age of the 1950s traveling salesman, sitting through those meetings. I had read how it was very important to form good relation-ships with these reps, as at the time, yarn demand was on the rise, and supply was tight. You needed the reps pulling for you inside the company, so you could get your yarn faster.

But it wasn't easy.

I learned that the yarn reps would generally go out on calls twice a year, after the suppliers released their new yarns and colors for the spring, and again for the fall. They would offer you a very small window for a meeting—saying some-thing like "I'm coming next Tuesday; can you meet me at three P.M.?" And they would expect at least three hours for each meeting.

When the reps did arrive (often hours late), they would wheel in several suitcases of yarn. After looking over what was on our shelves and chitchatting about how our sales were going, "the show" would begin.

One by one, they would pull out the new yarns for the season, and the patterns that went with the yarn. There would be a heavy sales pitch for each yarn, often so trans-parently transactional, it was like sitting ringside at a circus:

"*This* is the must-have yarn of the season!"

"The last store I went to bought *three* bags in every color!"

"*All* of your customers will be asking for this!"

"The other guys say they have this, but theirs is *junk*!"

"If you buy the whole line, we'll send you this sweater model *free*!"

Often I honestly had to work hard to keep a straight face. If I'd ever tried to pitch one of our branding clients with an approach like this, I would have been laughed out the door. Part of me was insulted that they would use these blatantly disingenuous, strong-arm tactics on me. Did this actually *work* on other yarn store owners? Did people really fall for this? When I thought of all those other, unsuspecting owners who didn't have my branding background, it made me really angry.

But at the same time, I recognized that these reps were doing the best they could with the tools and training they had been given. I worked hard to break through the B.S. and establish a real rapport with them. In doing so, I found out that many of these yarn companies were just distributorships, run by people (again, mostly men) who didn't knit. It was a commodity to them, a business, nothing more.

But the more I got to know the reps, the more I saw an opportunity—to work with them as allies, to learn about trends affecting the industry from a 10,000-foot view.

I pulled out my metaphorical empathy hat, gifted to me so many years ago by my dad, and put it on.

I empathized with their challenges: being on the road, week after week, and dealing with yarn store owners who, for the most part, had very little business background. I heard horror stories from reps who drove days to meet with owners who often canceled at the last minute. It was apparently the norm for owners not to return calls or e-mails, or to blackball a rep because the owner didn't like the policies of the yarn company, or because a shipment had arrived late, or just . . . because. Often the reps would be sent out on the road without complete information on the yarn lines they were supposed to be selling.

I started making more time to talk to each rep—sharing about family, hopes, and dreams. I got really transparent about my goals for Loops. I wanted the reps to understand the thinking behind the yarn choices we made. Over time, the chatty beginning of each meeting got longer, while the meat of the meeting—the buying process itself—got shorter, as I became more and more direct with my opinions, and faster with my decisions.

To quote author and speaker Brené Brown: "Clear is kind. Unclear is unkind." This is never more true than in a yarn buying appointment! Letting these reps run through a whole song and dance, allowing them to wax on about the properties of a yarn that I knew I didn't want or need, was a waste of their time and ultimately, unkind. The clearer I could be with a rep about what our needs were, about what I liked and didn't like, the more efficient and productive our meetings would be.

A friend of mine, Melinda, once shared a story about her father, a successful businessman who often met with vendors whose very livelihood might depend on the order he placed. At the end of every negotiation—whether a sales meeting with a vendor, a merger meeting with a partner, or anything in between—he would ask the same question:

"Is this a good deal for *you*?"

He knew that any successful business relationship depended on deals that are good for both sides. If the vendor undercuts himself to get the contract, he hurts himself in the long run. He might not be in business by the time the next selling season rolls around, and the relationship is lost. When there is a lopsided "win," you might feel good for a moment. But a lopsided win is not a win in the long run.

Maintaining empathetic, equitable relationships with everyone—your team, your partners, and your vendors—is more than the right thing to do. It's the smart thing to do.

CHAPTER 18

GETTING SOCIAL

Since Branders, Inc. continued to bring in 100 percent more income than Loops, I continued to wear both hats. In between writing ads for banks and oil companies and casinos, I got to write ads and promotions for Loops. It was a complete blast to develop a brand voice from scratch—*my voice*—without any clients to answer to, other than the customers themselves.

I would savor the little blocks of time that I would carve out to do this, often as a reward for finishing a particularly daunting task, like writing a brochure on an especially dry topic. I would sit down with a blank notepad and a favorite pen, and just let my freaky fiber flag fly.

The only problem was, I couldn't afford to place my awesome ads in traditional media.

I was determined that Loops had to "make it" on its own two feet, without borrowing money from our other business, or taking on investors. So the budget line item for Loops advertising was tiny. We could only afford to take out an ad in the *Tulsa World* a couple times a year, and those we reserved for big sale days. We did reach out to our contacts in the ad business, tried some unconventional publication ads, and even a small run on some inexpensive local billboards. But TV and radio were out of the question—way, way out.

My saving grace was the rise of a whole new phenomenon called social media.

I didn't really understand Facebook, but I knew one thing: it was free. What did it hurt to try? So I started experimenting with different types of posts. The conversational, transparent style, the storytelling and fun visuals that Facebook seemed to love—all came naturally to me. Day by day, I watched our numbers and engagement climb, often at a dizzying pace.

And then there was the groundbreaking new website called Ravelry. Founded in 2007 by two knitters who became frustrated by trying to find information about patterns and yarns, Ravelry was a revelation—a place to keep track of your stash, to find and download free and paid patterns, to get inspired, and to connect with yarn lovers around the world. And there were Ravelry forums for every imaginable interest, including forums for fans of individual designers . . . and forums for fans of specific yarn stores! Before our eyes, Ravelry rapidly ascended from a beta project to an award-winning site with more than 7 million users. Designers opened pattern stores on Ravelry, and whole businesses began to be built on the platform. A single successful pattern could take a designer from unknown to self-employed and self-sufficient overnight.

Plus, advertising on Ravelry, especially in the beginning, was ultra-cheap. You just had to be a little creative and a little adventurous.

Check, check, and check.

Another cool thing about social media was this: Nobody gave a hoot if you were in Tulsa, Oklahoma. We had found a way to break through the apparent Northeast–Northwest barrier that seemed to bar all the yarn stores located in states "in the middle" of the United States from playing in the sandbox. Knitters even seemed to find our midwestern vibe—*gasp*—refreshingly friendly!

Building on our early social media success, we created a new online store (loopsknitting.com), and managed to connect it to our in-store inventory, which was no small feat. You see, it's really important to a knitter to know exactly how many skeins of a given color you have in stock. So if you sell, say, two skeins in the store, and your online store doesn't reflect that sale fast enough, someone else might purchase eight skeins for a sweater online. Whoops! Then you have to e-mail the poor customer and let them know they're actually two skeins short of a sweater. Not a good customer experience. So for a brick-and-mortar yarn store with an online presence, it's crucial that all of the inventory—in-store and online—is synced up, in as close as possible to real time.

And the truth is, even without its special technological challenges, yarn is a fairly complex thing to sell online. A typical yarn store has hundreds or thousands of SKUs (stock keeping units), with all of the different types, brands, weights, and colors of fiber. This doesn't even take into consideration the huge variations that can happen from dye lot to dye lot!

And needles . . . well, every knitter knows that you can never have enough needles. Even a single brand of needles can include hundreds of sizes: circumferences from size 00 through 50, and lengths from 6 to 60 inches. Then add in straight needles, circular needles, interchangeable needles, double-pointed needles, different woods and metals, round and square . . . well, shoot, you could have a 10,000-square-foot store filled with only needles.

We saw, early on, that Loops could never be the Amazon or Walmart of yarn. We weren't tech-savvy or big enough to compete on price. Where we *could* shine was in our curation and our service. Our secret sauce was our ability to pair the perfect yarn with the perfect project—with a focus on on-trend, effortless designs—and then back it up with the same level of support you would get from a good friend who's been knitting and crocheting all her life. The Loops customer was the fashion-forward knitter or crocheter who didn't want to waste time *looking* for beautiful, creative projects in super-soft yarn; she just wanted to enjoy *making* them, then finish, wear, or gift them!

I've been driving the Loopsmobile since 2012. I knit the swatch;
Brent scanned it and designed the wrap.

Basically, we wanted our online store to be the Hot Loops Wall experience, brought to life on your computer.

It was definitely a David vs. Goliath strategy. But get this . . . it started to work!

Our online presence began to grow. The first year we established the online store, it was around 1 percent of Loops's total sales. The next year, it was 5 percent. When we attended trade shows, we were surprised when yarn vendors and other yarn stores from across the country suddenly recognized "Loops" on our nametags. We were gaining a following? Perhaps even becoming just a little bit "yarn famous"? Maybe, just maybe, all that time experimenting with Facebook and Ravelry, the countless hours wrestling with unfamiliar tech to build the website, were all about to pay off.

CHAPTER 19

KNOWING YOUR WORTH

When I was working at O'Neil, my first ad agency job out of college, I started at a whopping $12,000 a year. But I had to move out of my mom's house, so, I found a barely habitable apartment at a complex called the Glens, in the highest-crime area of Tulsa.

I hauled my childhood mattress up to the second floor and into my bedroom, bought a $300 couch with big floral pillows from the local mega-furniture store on layaway, and set up my first apartment. It wasn't the kind of place you were eager to come home to, so I got in the habit of working late, going straight to Jazzercise, then coming home, showering, slurping up some of the aforementioned ramen noodles, collapsing into sleep . . . then rising early to get to work and make more ads.

It was a nail-biter each month to pay the electric bill, much less purchase luxuries like work-appropriate clothes, eat out, or buy gas to drive anywhere beyond Jenks. Within just a few months, I realized I wasn't going to be able to make ends meet. My salary wasn't sustainable, even in a relatively affordable city like Tulsa. And moving back home was not an option.

I explained my predicament to Hotshot.

"I know, it's a ridiculous salary, but it's all I could get out of O'Neil when I talked him into hiring you," he said. "You're just gonna have to march in there to him and tell him why you deserve more money."

Hmmmm. How does a 23-year-old who's been at a job only six months prove that she's worth more? Then inspiration struck: The Job List.

I grabbed the latest O'Neil Job List and started highlighting all the jobs that had my initials by them. To my great surprise, almost 80 percent of the jobs were flagged with my initials, SV! Granted, the jobs assigned to Hotshot and the other senior writer were much bigger and more important to the firm, but *still*. I had my ammunition.

Armed with the highlighted Job List and marching as best I could in my cheap black pumps, I headed into the CEO's office . . . and walked out with a $3,000 raise.

Over the next year, I would march in and out of that same office three more times, until I was finally earning enough to graduate from ramen noodles to Lean Cuisines and could afford to add a second skirt to my work wardrobe.

Through the years, I was always really surprised by my creative colleagues' reluctance to advocate for themselves financially. They would fight tooth and nail for a creative concept but do almost anything to avoid a conversation about a change in compensation, or title, or even an office with decent lighting that allows them to produce better-quality design. Even though, in a branding business, the ideas *are* the product. From that day until now, there exists this misguided thinking that discussing money and growth opportunities somehow cheapens the artist. The romantic "ideal" of the starving artist is alive and well, and still doing a great disservice to creatives of all types, everywhere, who strive to build a career or a business based on their own creative currency.

I get it. It can be terrifying to put yourself out there—not only to put your innermost creative expressions out on display for the world to see, but to have the seeming audacity for others to pay you what you're really worth. The vulnerability is compounded exponentially.

It's so tempting to lower the price of that course or that membership or that painting. To charge next to nothing for that handknit piece "because I just did it while I was watching TV." To accept that contract for less than your published hourly rate, because it's a "sure thing" and will take some pressure off you to perform at your best.

We convince ourselves that by accepting a lower value for our work, we'll increase our own margin of error, and that anvil will be less likely to fall on our heads.

Despite the fact that I advocated to get all of those raises, since then I've definitely had my share of moments when I succumbed to this faulty line of thinking.

Loops was *seven years old* before I took my first owner's draw. I just kept pouring all the money back into the business, in the mistaken belief that I somehow didn't deserve to pay myself first. That my contribution wasn't enough. That the other employees would somehow find out and judge me, thinking that if I wasn't behind the counter selling yarn, if I was at home working on research and purchase orders and financials and e-mails and Facebook posts, I wasn't really working.

It wasn't until someone pointed out to me that, from any outside perspective, the business wouldn't really have value until I could demonstrate that it could support my salary, that I finally began to take one—a very, very small one—but with regularity that I could build on.

And if I had never taken that first step, hadn't decided to stop "playing small," I would never have been able to transition fully from the branding business to the yarn business, many years later.

Similarly, there came a point in Loops's growth that I considered lowering prices below MSRP (Manufacturer's Suggested Retail Price), so that I could compete in the big red ocean of online yarn sales, where all the big players seemed to be engrossed in a race to the bottom, constantly undercutting one another. At that point, I made a conscious decision to go in the other direction, to become a premium brand focused on high-touch customer experience, exclusive products, and trusted curation.

This gave me the freedom to set prices that were fair to the consumer *and* appropriate to the value of the product. I could support the independent yarn dyers with agreements that were good *for both of us*, without the need to wield buying power to squeeze them into contracts they were uncomfortable with. I could stop having discounts and sales reactively, and choose to offer them proactively, as an intentional way to reward our loyal customers.

Today, when I connect with creative people who are wrestling with how to value themselves and their work—whether they're opening their first Etsy shop or offering their first online product—the conversation almost always includes me encouraging them to really see their value, urging them to take a salary from the start, or to raise their initial prices.

If you undervalue yourself, I tell them, how can you expect your audience to really appreciate your worth? Money—salary, raises, retail prices, commissions for custom work—it's all a form of appreciation. Maybe you don't need the money right now. Maybe you can get by on less. But please, get really honest with yourself here: As a working creative, you *do* need the appreciation. It's a form of connection. And like water and sunshine for plants, for us humans and especially for us creatives, it's absolutely critical. We all need—*must have*—that connection to stay inspired, to thrive, and to keep moving forward.

WHAT TO REMEMBER AS YOU MOVE AHEAD . . .

Progress, not perfection. From the very beginning, set aside any perfectionism. It will not serve you—neither as a knitter nor as a creative entrepreneur. Make small goals, then take the time to recognize and celebrate when you meet them. Feeling overwhelmed? Make the goals smaller. Ask yourself, what is the smallest possible step I can take toward my goals today? Maybe it's writing one word. Making one stitch. Some days, maybe it's just getting out of bed. Acknowledge that *any* progress is just that—progress.

You have more energy than you realize. The human capacity for endurance and achievement is boundless. You have deep wells of energy inside you that have yet to be tapped. When life comes out of nowhere and bitch-slaps you, when fear takes over and your mind is spinning and you can't imagine a future let alone how you will get through this day, know that this too shall pass. And what's more, "this" has the potential to become the catalyst for your greatest contribution, for the dream you haven't even begun to dream yet.

Padlock your resolve. Before you begin your journey or take the next step, dig deep. Muster all of that strength lurking inside you. Put your plan, your vision, and your big audacious goals into words and write them down, then hang them up somewhere you can refer to them again and again. Take that resolve and make it real. Lock it in and throw away the key. So when it is tested—and trust me, it will be, over and over again—you'll always have a place to come back to and stoke the fire that got you started in the first place.

Make sure it's a good deal for everyone. The seemingly insignificant deal you make today might become the seed that grows into the partnership that defines your career. This is one of the most important ways you can exercise your empathy muscle. Put yourself in their shoes first, then take action accordingly.

Advocate for yourself. When you ask for that raise, or raise that price, you're committing an act of self-acceptance. Every single time the boss grants that raise, or the customer pays that price, it's validating not just your worth, but your creativity. That validation feeds further creativity. Words flow. Stitches fly. The creative fire is stoked, again and again and again. Don't douse your own spark before it even has the chance to catch.

Your Third Move

WHEN
THINGS
UNRAVEL

CHAPTER 20

THE FROG POND

Many knitters live in fear of something we call "frogging."

This is knitter's slang for when things go really wrong, and you realize you've made a mistake so significant that you need to unravel or "rip" your work all the way back to where the mistake occurred. Often, you get a gut feeling that something is wrong, but you keep going, afraid to look back and see the problem that your gut is telling you is there.

When you finally see and acknowledge the mistake, you have to "rip-it, rip-it"—sounds like a frog's "ribbit, ribbit"—and unravel it all the way back to the error, undoing hours or even weeks' worth of effort. That's why you'll hear many knitters say how much they dread a trip to the frog pond.

But, as knitters progress in their journey, they are surprised to discover that there can be so much value in the frogging itself. In the act of unraveling and re-knitting. In fact, the very process can also teach you a great deal, if you let it—about the anatomy of the stitches, about how they intertwine to create the fabric, about how you might improve your technique, and most of all, about patience.

These are things you might never learn, might never grow from, if you never encounter the difficulty in the first place.

The summer after my first internship with the Ford Agency, I landed an even more coveted internship—with a large, Tulsa-based production company whose primary client was ESPN.

When, while on spring break from TCU, I walked through this company's imposing doors for my interview, I was thoroughly intimidated. If the Ford Agency had been a female nirvana, this was the ultimate man cave. High ceilings, glass, chrome, and original LeRoy Neiman impressionist paintings were everywhere. In huge, dark suites, editors sat surrounded by screens and equipment, while clients lounged on the big leather sectionals, sipping (or more accurately, chugging) martinis.

Toward the back of the main floor, there was a little sign for a tiny ad agency that was wholly owned by the company. My understanding was that the owner had gotten fed up with his contracted ad agency, and just decided to make his own. It currently consisted of one employee, a self-professed creative director I'll call John.

As I bopped my sophomore self into John's office with a huge, eager smile on my face, he quickly scanned me up and down through his yellow-tinted glasses. I felt my smile fade a little as I suppressed an involuntary shudder. Was it just me . . . or was he checking me out? Surely not. He was a professional. And he was *old*. I pushed down the discomfort and started to pull out my portfolio.

"How old are you?" was John's first question.

As I lowered my eyes and quickly answered "Nineteen" before pivoting to a discussion of my portfolio and writing experience, I felt his eyes on me—not my portfolio. The interview lasted more than an hour. Every warning bell I had was going off, full-blast, as he kept changing the subject from my questions about the job to his questions about my life in college, my hobbies, my boyfriend.

"In this department it will be just the two of us . . . and if I'm going to take the time to teach you, I want to make sure we work well together," he said.

Again, my gut was screaming *RUN*. But it was such an incredible opportunity. And there would be all of these other people around. Surely I was reading the signals wrong? Surely I would spend most of my time at my desk, creating, and I could control the situation? Surely it was my imagination that, as I left that day, I smelled alcohol on John's breath?

Just when I was starting to hope I *didn't* get the job . . . I got it.

From a learning perspective, the internship turned out to be a tremendous experience. As I proved my writing capability, I got to work on more and more accounts. My portfolio grew by leaps and bounds. How could I complain, when I was adding clients like ESPN to my résumé?

But all of this education definitely came at a price—and with some lessons that I didn't think I would ever have to learn.

John was clearly day drinking, more and more. He was gone for long stretches at a time—which was fine with me— because it meant I had more assignments and could get more done. But when he *was* in the office, the main lesson I was learning was how to bob and weave.

He would call me into his office and shut the door. Often, he would begin by complaining about something—the boss, some jerk in traffic on his way to work, his ex. I would change the subject to a project I was working on, trying to get him to focus on the concept or an edit I was struggling with. These rallies would go back and forth, with me always guiding the topic back to work, and John always pushing toward more intimate subjects.

Sometimes he would start telling personal stories and the minutes would turn into hours. Often I'd look away, out into the hall or down at the papers in my lap . . . and feel his eyes on me. So creepy. Other times, while working at my desk, I'd feel that stare and look up and out the doorway to see him standing across the hall, just watching me.

If you're reading this and waiting for the "#MeToo" shoe to drop, it didn't, not exactly. There was never any huge moment where he came in for a kiss or a grab. Luckily for me, he was too smart for that.

There was just this constant discomfort—every moment of every workday. Like that feeling when you make a wrong turn into a dark alley, and you need to move your keys in your hands so that the big key is pointing outward, weaponized. Your eyes widen and your pulse quickens and you're on high alert.

I learned that being creative—*while* bobbing and weaving—is exhausting. Some might say it toughened me up, made me a better writer, especially under pressure. Maybe it did.

But a few months later, when the summer internship was long over, and I was back home in Tulsa for winter break, I got a call on my princess-style home phone.

"Hi, Shelley, it's John," said the voice.

He went on to tell me that all summer, he'd wanted to ask me out, but as my boss, he felt he needed to be professional.

"Now that you don't work for my company, I'd kick myself if I didn't at least try."

He was in his 40s. I was 19.

I felt sick.

All the warnings, all the feelings I'd convinced myself were my imagination—it was all real. And worst of all, it made me doubt my talent. Had he really seen something special in my portfolio when I interviewed? Had my writing really gotten better over the summer? Or had he just been hoping for some illicit romance all along?

I told him I had a boyfriend and politely declined.

And then I went to the bathroom and threw up.

From that day on, I knew that if I was going to continue in the *Mad Men*'s world of advertising, I'd better learn to pay closer attention to my gut. No matter how dazzling the opportunity, no matter how eager I was to progress in my career, even when on the surface all the stitches seemed to be coming together . . . when that little voice started chirping at me that something was off, I needed to tune in and listen.

Three years later, when I was working at O'Neil, I had my first chance to apply what I'd learned from the John experience. One day, a really important client that I had never met was due to visit the office. I had convinced the owner of the company, who managed this particular account, to let me sit in on the meeting.

I heard the client arrive, heard the owner exchange pleasantries with him, heard them approaching. I stood up to meet the client.

"Shelley, this is Mr. Client. Mr. Client, meet Shelley. She's a recent graduate of TCU, a Horned Frog, and a darn good writer.

"Around here, we call her Shelley Goodbody."

WHAT did he just call me? I thought.

I felt my face go tomato-red. I hadn't felt a blush so deep since middle school. Did my boss, the owner of the company, really just introduce me to a client that way? As I struggled to regain my composure, I realized they were both having a really good chuckle and looking at me like I should be flattered.

I wasn't able to say much in that meeting. I smiled, nodded, and thought, *Just let this be over.* But it didn't stop there. The next time a male client came in for a meeting (I had started to notice, as a matter of fact, that *all* of the clients were male), the owner introduced me the same way again.

This time, I was listening to my gut, and I was prepared. I offered the client a handshake. I looked him straight in the eye and said, "You can call me Shelley." Then I gave the owner a pointed look and a confident smile.

That meeting went much better.

And just like that, my "nickname" was a thing of the past.

I resolved to keep my eyes and ears open in the future, and at the earliest sign of that queasy feeling in my gut, to stand up and speak out. While I had no problem advocating for my creative ideas, I found it much more difficult to acknowledge and call out issues of covert and overt sexism. But I'd learned how ignoring the problem could poison the entire experience—or to put it in knitting terms, it could make me want to just abandon the whole project and never return to it again.

This, I knew, was a necessary unraveling. A critical unlearning and re-knitting. I knew it was a muscle that I must continue to train, until it became second nature to flex.

CHAPTER 21

GET THIS LITTLE GIRL OFF MY ACCOUNT

At Ad Inc, after proving myself on the Oklahoma Natural Gas account, I'd begun to also work on the Thrifty Car Rental account, and I was really enjoying it. I was added to Thrifty as a secondary writer. The primary writer, Steve, handled most of the big jobs, and I the less important ones. But slowly, I began to work my way up to bigger and bigger assignments. And they began to have an impact—first, with accolades at our local ADDY awards show. And then, in the way of actual impact on the bottom line of the company.

My ads were moving the needle—for a national car rental company.

So cool. Right?

Well, mostly cool. The only bummer was, the client had no idea that I was working on his ads. Even on the ADDY award credits, only the primary writer's name was listed. My name was noticeably absent.

I asked Dorcas about it, and she explained that Ted, the Ad Inc executive in charge of the Thrifty account, didn't think the client would be comfortable with having more than one writer.

And because Ted was also the president of Ad Inc, we both knew it was wiser not to fight it.

But I *did* persist in my requests to get included in the client meetings. I wanted to know more about the car rental experience, the pain points and aspirations of the ideal car rental customer. If I could get into just one meeting, I knew I could make the ad campaigns even more successful.

Finally, my chance arrived. There was going to be a meeting of the entire Thrifty team—a big presentation of a campaign that I had been instrumental in concepting and writing. I'd worked with a new, female art director, just a few years older than me, who had just joined Ad Inc. We weren't the primary team—but the project was so critical that Ted had decided to bring "all hands on deck." Three separate creative teams (each comprised of one writer and one designer) had been formed to come up with independent concepts.

Rose and I were sort of the "flyer team"—no one really expected us to have the winning concept. So we decided to go wild. What was there to lose, really?

Our ads didn't have a single picture of a car. Instead, the first ad had a giant photo of Imelda Marcos's face, with a headline about shoes. I didn't really know the term for it then, but this ad was a "pattern interrupt," aimed at getting the attention of the growing audience of female executives who rented cars for business trips.

Shockingly, the account team was really excited about our concepts! It was decided that all of the creative teams would come to the meeting, to make a big show for the client of how much effort the agency had put into the campaign.

I remember going into Dorcas's office before the meeting was about to start. I told her I was freaking out—I was so nervous! I asked how she had developed her nerves of steel for big meetings, and she said something I've never forgotten. I still think of it before going live or giving a talk.

"Oh please, nerves of steel?" She laughed. "Let me tell you something. Before every big client presentation, look for my pumps under the stall in the bathroom—I'll be in there throwing up! And then I'll walk into that meeting and knock it out of the park. You're going to do the same—hopefully minus the throwing up."

Knowing that someone like Dorcas, with all her confidence and decades of experience, still got nervous before big meetings, was somehow incredibly empowering.

So, armed with all the confidence of a 20-something with a great campaign under her belt, I headed into the meeting (thankfully, I skipped the bathroom part).

The large, impressive, dark-wooded conference room with big leather swivel chairs was filling up fast. It had been decided that the account team would present all the concepts, along with Todd, the executive creative director. The rest of us were to sit there attentively, and essentially provide tonnage of bodies—lots of butts in seats—to indicate the massive amount of time and effort Ad Inc had put into the project. I figured this was all to help sell the sizable monthly retainer the client was paying. But, as I was about to find out, it was more about the client's ego than anything else.

Mr. Thrifty entered the building, surrounded by a team of assistants. I heard him bellow at the receptionist, then watched him barge into the room. I'd never met him before, but I had heard many tales. And Mr. Thrifty was instantly identifiable as a bark-bellow-barge kind of fellow.

The room fell silent.

Ted stood up, cleared his throat, and began the presentation. There was the "setup"—the challenge at hand, the target audience, the key message the campaign needed to convey. Then Todd stood up and tried cracking a couple of car rental jokes, but they weren't seeming to land with Mr.

Thrifty. Everything about this client's posture said, "Get on with it. Get to the goods."

So Todd pulled out an enormous pile of presentation boards—thick, heavy, matte black boards with different ad layouts, which had been painstakingly mounted to the boards with the careful use of rulers and spray adhesive.

He started with the ads from the number-one creative team—the two oldest guys. Big pictures of shiny cars, large bold headlines, copy about excellent value and smooth service. Mr. Thrifty remained silent, stony, and expressionless as Todd moved on to the next campaign, and the next. Finally, he got to our Imelda Marcos ad, at the bottom of the stack.

"This one is really just a wild card—we wanted you to see how far out of the box we could go."

Mr. Thrifty's eyebrows raised, ever so slightly.

"That one is interesting," he said. "Do you have more of those?" We did. Two more ads, even more outlandish than the first.

"I like it," Mr. Thrifty declared.

"Really?" Todd sputtered. "Th-that's fantastic!"

You could feel the palpable shock ripple through the room.

"Who wrote this one?" Mr. Thrifty inquired.

Oh no. Oh no oh no oh no, everyone is looking at ME! *Okay, Shelley . . . stay calm. You got this.*

I raised my hand, just a little. "I did. Rose and I worked on it together." His head slowly swiveled in my direction. "Who is THIS?" he demanded of the room.

"I'm Shelley. I've actually been working on your account for the last year." I went on to mention a couple of the ads I'd written that had earned awards and resulted in significant sales upticks.

The room fell silent as a seemingly endless pregnant pause ensued. I could see Mr. Thrifty mulling over this new information. I'm not sure what I was expecting next—maybe a "Thank you" or a "Wow, you're really talented" or even possibly "Give this woman a raise!"

Instead, I got a shock I'll never forget. Mr. Thrifty turned to Todd and said, with great finality: "The campaign is great, we're going with it.

"But get this *little girl* off my account. She's not even old enough to rent a car."

This was certainly a Frog Pond moment.

It felt like I'd taken a giant step back ("Mother, may I? NO YOU MAY NOT.")

But looking back, that day in the boardroom with Mr. Thrifty was a gift. A chance to unravel a bit, examine my progress, and begin again.

This was the day I began thinking seriously about starting my own copywriting business.

TRIAGE

The Sunday before we were set to open the first Loops store in Utica Square, I was at the store, trying to hook up the new computer, when I got a phone call. It wasn't a great connection, and I thought I must be hearing incorrectly. The crackly voice on the other end announced himself as an EMSA (ambulance) driver.

"Shelley Brander?"

"Yes . . . "

"We have your husband en route to St. Francis; please meet us at the hospital."

I flew out of Loops, vaulted into my car and dashed down the highway, telling myself slow down, you can't get into a wreck right before the store opens!

I got to the hospital, breathlessly asked to see Brent Brander . . .

. . . and got nothing but a quizzical look in return.

"We don't have a Brent Brander," the nurse at the triage desk said.

I was starting to really panic now, worrying there was something they weren't telling me. "But they just called me from the ambulance! He has to be here somewhere."

The nurse picked up the phone and made more calls. She kept stealing worried glances at me, suggesting that maybe I wanted to sit down? But I was really freaking out now.

Just when I'd convinced myself that Brent was dying in a basement somewhere, alone and forgotten, the nurse announced, "Found him!"

Brent had been playing tennis at Indian Springs Country Club, in Broken Arrow, a suburb of Tulsa. He had been picked up by a *Broken Arrow EMSA* ambulance, and taken to *St. Francis South*, a brand-new location that had just opened. Thus the confusion.

Once I was able to get to the right hospital, I learned the full story. Brent had been in a third set tiebreaker of a doubles match and had begun to have chest pains. Luckily, one of his opponents was a cardiac surgeon who immediately recognized the signs of atrial fibrillation, or AFib. At first, Brent had been suspicious that the doctor was just trying to get Brent to quit so he could win the match! But finally, the pain spreading up his neck, Brent became convinced it was real and allowed himself to default the match and succumb to the ambulance ride.

It turned out that Brent had sky-high blood pressure, which we later found out was caused by his undiagnosed sleep apnea. If he couldn't come out of the AFib on his own by the next morning, they would have to try shocking his heart back into the right rhythm.

Around 5 A.M., I awoke in my chair next to Brent's hospital bed to the piercing sound of an alarm. All the machines were blinking with red lights and once again, I panicked . . . until a nurse arrived and said his blood pressure had actually dropped too *low* . . . and it looked like that had reset his heart to a natural rhythm, all on its own.

Hugely relieved, we headed home. And even though this experience was obviously terrifying for Brent, he knew he was lucky that it had uncovered the underlying issue.

For me, it turned out to be a great reset from the universe.

It was time for a different kind of triage, the kind where I took stock of my priorities and put my family first.

I could see how consumed I'd become with getting the first Loops opened. Inventory and shelving and employees and marketing occupied every moment of my day. When was the last time I had stopped to share a meal with my family? When was the last time Brent and I had had a conversation about something other than business?

On this pivotal day, I'd been reminded that, no matter what was going on in our businesses, it could all come crashing down in an instant if we didn't have our health, if we didn't have each other. What good was selling a bunch of yarn if I wasn't there for my family when they needed me? What good was having big branding accounts that helped fund my kids' education, if it left me no time to read books with my children and sing them to sleep each night?

CHAPTER 23

NORTH VS. SOUTH

Like so many epic failures, it seemed to make so much sense at the time.

In 2012, Loops was six years old, and even though the store was doing well and the online sales were growing, I had yet to take a salary. I was still working both the Loops and the Branders business with Brent, and something had to give. I needed to find a way for Loops to expand and create enough cash flow that I could leave the branding business.

At that time, Tulsa was essentially divided in half by a major road construction project, widening the east–west interstate highway that bisected the city. To make matters worse, it seemed that every significant, arterial north–south street was under construction, as well. The congestion was a mess.

Tulsa had become a Tale of Two Cities: Midtown/North Tulsa and South Tulsa. People on the north side of I-44 didn't want to cross it going south. And people on the south side didn't want to cross it going north. Tulsa knitters, like all other Tulsans, had very strong opinions about this. Heated discussions would often erupt in the store. We started getting more and more requests to build "a south store" to serve the ever-expanding suburbia on the other side of I-44, many of whom were ordering from us online just so they didn't have to drive more than 10 minutes and cross the construction barrier.

It seemed the ideal opportunity to test out my dream of multiple stores and eventual franchising. My idea was to create a second store, on the south side of Tulsa, with future franchising in mind: Everything documented, systemized, and easy to scale.

Creatively, what excited me the most was the opportunity to design the store from a "white box"—unencumbered by a pre-set layout or décor. At our Utica location, I knew I had been lucky to inherit a space designed by an interior decorator, one married to a world-renowned architect. But her French country aesthetic didn't exactly jibe with my personal vision for my yarn store: wide open spaces, clean contemporary design, and lots of white space to serve as the neutral background for the full spectrum of yarn colors and textures.

We found the perfect space for Loops South, in a new-ish, upscale strip center in South Tulsa. I reached out to my friend Phara, a customer, knitter, and interior designer whose star was on the rise (she had recently begun to work with Blake Shelton and Miranda Lambert), and whose style I loved. Phara said she would help out with some high-level oversight, but her time was mostly taken up, building music-star mansions. So she suggested a brilliant idea: approach a local university and see if they would partner with us, pro bono.

It worked! I contacted the Oklahoma State University interior design department, and a professor decided to make Loops South their graduate project for the semester. The students divided into teams, and each team developed and presented a store design concept. Watching each team present their designs was a highlight of the whole Loops South experience. They completely pushed the boundaries of what I imagined might be possible with a simple shotgun-style 2,000-square-foot space.

One all-male team conceived a design that was less store, more man cave. "The husbands need a cool place to hang out while the wives shop," they said. Their drawings included a huge TV, recliners, even a wet bar! Yeah, it was little over the top but inspiring nonetheless. Because of these students' ideas, we resolved to have at least a small "yarn husband" waiting area in Loops South with comfy chairs, magazines, and video games.

In the end, we implemented a myriad of design elements from the OSU teams. Most notable were a circular cash-wrap checkout area surrounded by barstools, with a lighted floating ceiling element that echoed that loop shape (and resembled a cool flying saucer); and a space-aged display of buttons created with wood, plaster, and clothes dryer vent tubing.

The design of the second Loops location was inspired by concepts from design students from Oklahoma State University.

We kept other key elements that had become part of the Loops lexicon but streamlined them so they could be replicated in future franchise stores. There was a dedicated playroom with a floor-to-ceiling blackboard for doodling, a classroom with a magnetic wall where customers could pin up photos of their recently finished projects, and pristine, white cubbies lining the walls. As for the Hot Loops Wall? Rather than custom-built shelving, we figured out how to adapt IKEA shelving to our Hot Loops concept, incorporating finished photos of the projects.

Button display fashioned from wood and venting for clothes dryers.

Loops South: Belly up to the yarn bar!

Opening day of the second Loops location, "Loops South."

While the construction crew got to work, building out our dream store design, we focused on solving another challenge: how to combine the inventory of both locations onto our single website. We knew it was critical for our customers to be able to shop the inventory of both stores at once. If there were four skeins of Malabrigo Rios in Ravelry Red available at the Utica store, and six skeins at the South store, but the customer needed eight skeins for her sweater, the site had to show all 10 skeins in stock—if she couldn't order enough, she would move on to another site.

"No problem," said the team at POSIM, our point-of-sale and website provider. "We got you."

Except, as it turned out, they didn't get us. Not at all.

The week before our South store grand opening, as we were stocking shelves, putting all the final touches on the marketing, and getting our new team members trained, we got the news.

"We're sorry," said our POSIM project manager. "The integration is not working."

I took a very deep breath.

"No problem. We'll just delay the online announcement until you figure out the workaround," I said.

"No, you don't understand. The integration *will not work.* It's just not possible. Your site will only be able to reflect the inventory of one store or the other. Not both."

Deeper breath.

I asked to meet with the top developers at the company, and after that, even the owners, but there was no solution. Our website would be limited to showing only about half of our total inventory. While this was a devastating blow, at this point there was no turning back. Loops South would open as planned.

And, website woes aside, the opening of Loops South was a smashing success.

The Southside customers were ecstatic to have a modern yarn store so nearby. And even the Northside customers made grudging trips across the orange-cone construction divide to see what all the fuss was about.

We intentionally stocked each store with yarns and featured projects that were unique to each location. We wanted customers to visit *both* stores, to see what was new. And, while each store had its own manager and team, we decided that some Loops Troops would float between locations—myself included. The idea was to have continuity across the brand, but with each location expressing its own unique personality.

Best. Laid. Plans.

The first couple of years for Loops South seemed to bode well for the company. Despite POSIM's continued inability to overcome the website problem, sales were on the rise. Two stores didn't *quite* mean double the profits, but things were headed in the right direction. I was able to start taking small, regular draws. Not enough to leave the branding business—not by a longshot. But Loops South was definitely holding its own.

And there was a side benefit I hadn't anticipated. Our opening a second store had apparently sent a ripple through the industry. When we showed up at our next national trade show, every vendor seemed to know about Loops South. "You started a second store? In *Tulsa*?" they would ask incredulously. Having two stores not only gave us more buying strength in terms of quantity, but also in terms of a sort of star status. There was no denying it: People were talking about Loops.

This honestly made me a little uncomfortable at first. I realized I kind of liked being under the radar, slipping along from booth to booth, being able to shop the merchandise without being bombarded. I was glad I'd brought some

Loops Troops along, so that they could shop more anonymously, while I assumed the PR role of explaining our new store concept, working out trunk show agreements, and generally building relationships.

Being invited to be one of the participating shops for the 2014
Stephen & Steven Tour was a turning point for Loops.

It also became much easier to attract and book big-name designers for workshops and other events. In fact, *they* started to come to *us*. Most notable was when we were invited to be part of the 2012 Stephen & Steven Tour. Stephen West was a young, fabulous knitwear designer living in Amsterdam (but, believe it or not, originally from Tulsa!) and Steven Berg was a menswear-designer-turned-yarn-mogul with an over-the-top rock star aesthetic, a chandelier-laden yarn shop in Minneapolis, and an entourage who traveled with him wherever he went. They had paired up for a dynamic-duo tour and invited Loops to be one of the lucky host stores! We were over the moon to be included alongside a dozen of the top yarn stores in North America.

The event was a ginormous hit, and Loops South sales skyrocketed—not just during the event, but for many months afterward.

But underneath the sparkly surface of Loops's success, there was starting to be some fraying at the edges.

Two factions had begun to form. North vs. South.

The Utica location, managed by Gina Y., was always calling over to the South location, managed by our original Gina H. The Ginas were good personal friends, but some tension had begun to grow around the issue of inventory. Basically, each Gina wanted the best yarns moved to her location. We were constantly shipping yarn back and forth, not necessarily to benefit the customer, but because one store was sure they could sell it better than the other.

Our former team mindset—one for all and all for one—began to become divided.

My attention became divided too.

Prior to opening Loops South, we had moved our family to a new home in South Tulsa. This made sense because our kids were now attending schools farther south. Since Loops South was the "new baby," and now just a five-minute drive away, it was where I tended to spend more and more of my Loops time. So the South employees, as well as the South customers, had my ear. It was subtle, and I even denied it . . . but in retrospect, it was clear that my decisions were rooted in what was best for the South store.

I tried to visit the Utica store at least twice a week, but I had a growing sense that I was losing control there. Gina Y. was a wonderful salesperson and had a natural ability to develop trust and friendship with her customers. But without realizing it, I think she started to form a customer faction that had an increasingly negative view of the other store.

And there's no delicate way to put this: the Utica store started to look shabby. While Gina H. was naturally gifted in store displays and neatness, it was not one of Gina Y's best strengths. She relied on other employees—especially one team member named Holly—to keep things looking organized and appealing, while she focused on taking care of the customers. But Holly's side hustle, a knitting-bag company called Binkwaffle, had started to grow rapidly, and she was less and less available to work the store. And as a result, Loops Utica suffered aesthetically. Each time I would walk in the door, my heart would hurt a little at what I saw as a decaying vibe. I would roll up my sleeves and spend a couple hours tidying up, which I'm sure was deflating to Gina Y., but I couldn't help myself.

At our monthly manager meetings, the tension became more and more palpable between North and South. Sometimes outright arguments would erupt, almost always over yarn. Which store would get which new yarn first? Which store was selling more, and why? Without adequate experience or training in managing a team, I almost always felt I handled these meetings poorly. I wanted both stores to shine equally. I wanted to make everyone happy.

I wanted the impossible.

And just as it started to sink in that things might be headed in the wrong direction, I had the worst day of my life.

CHAPTER 24

UNRAVELING

While all this North-vs.-South store drama was unfolding, the kids were growing up fast—as kids will do.

Sam (age 6), Cecily (age 5), Mallory (age 2).

While Mallory was humming along in Montessori school, Sam and Cecily had matriculated to a new middle school. It was a really tough move for both of them. Sam always struggled with major transitions, and the 8th-grade kids at his new school were a pretty tough crowd. (It was only years later that we discovered the extent of the bullying he endured.)

Cecily fared a bit better, because the 7th graders at the new school were nicer. And she loved the school's rock band program, that let her really shine as the brilliant percussionist she was becoming. Still, she had her own distinct challenges.

In 2nd grade, Cecily had finally been diagnosed with dyslexia, something I had suspected for years. But her preschool teacher had insisted that I was just comparing Cecily to Sam, who was hyperlexic (as are many kids on the autism spectrum). Sam had become so fixated on his alphabet toys as a toddler that we'd packed them all away. When Cec was finally diagnosed with dyslexia, I briefly blamed myself, thinking it was caused by depriving her of more access to those puzzles.

With the help of Ms. Renee, her alphabet phonics tutor, and a tremendous amount of dedication and hard work, Cecily was learning to cope with her challenges. She threw herself into her drumming and continually stunned us with her creativity. I would walk into the garage and find she had assembled a "trash drum set" using whatever she could find—paint cans and found metal, jar lids and junk she fished out of the recycling bin.

Her determination was boundless. She took up tennis, and quickly became the number-one player on her team. She took up cross-country running and was soon placing in the top finishers.

Cecily was also always kind to everyone, and helpful around the house. Despite the fact that her homework took her twice as long as her siblings, each night she would help me cook dinner, and even started helping me plan our family meals.

I had mentioned Cecily's love of meal-planning at our quarterly visit to the psychiatrist, who treated both Sam and Cecily for anxiety. I told him she seemed to be getting thinner, but that made sense, I guess, since she had started running cross-country.

The psychiatrist, who also happened to run one of the top eating disorder programs in the United States, put my mind at ease. "She's fine for her age, but if it makes you feel better, I can refer her to a nutritionist to help her stay fueled for cross-country, and to teach her good habits," he said. I set up the initial appointment.

And then one beautiful Sunday afternoon in the fall, Cecily and I decided to go for a walk with our one-year-old Lab puppy, Purl.

It was one of those days that begs you to be outside. The sunlight was dappling through the trees, and a light breeze was blowing. All of us were so happy to have this time together with no weekday deadlines, no pressures, no rush. Just a lazy, sunny Sunday afternoon spread out before us.

We put Purl on her little puppy leash and set out on our usual path through our gated neighborhood, from one end to the next. We paused at the back gate, debating for a moment whether to turn around. But it was such a nice day, and everyone (especially Purl!) wanted to keep going. So I clicked the clicker, the big steel gate swung open, and we walked through, into the neighborhood behind ours.

We had walked less than a block and were about to turn down the next street, when we heard shouting. We looked up to see a man and a woman, a few houses away, waving their arms and yelling what sounded like "No! Go back!"

My first thought was, "What? They can't they tell us where to go! It's a free country."

But in the next instant, I looked past them, into the adjacent yard, and saw two dogs that looked like oversized pit bulls. One was HUGE—at least 150 pounds. And they were headed straight toward us. Fast.

All at once I had 50 converging thoughts.

WHY didn't those shouting people stop their dogs . . . OH they weren't their dogs, they are trying to stop them . . . maybe we can outrun them . . . NO they're coming too fast . . . and now Purl had seen them and stopped in her tracks . . . QUICK give Cecily the clicker and tell her to . . . WALK but don't run, walk as fast as you can and get through the gate and shut it . . . OH GOOD Cecily is going to make it, maybe Purl and I can make it too . . . OH NO the dogs are way too fast, maybe they'll just want to play PLEASE GOD let them just want to play. . . .

And just like that, the dogs were upon us.

Things happened very, very fast from this point. To this day, part of the memory is lost, forever buried by a subconscious that would rather heal than remember.

The dogs sniffed at Purl, snarling. Smart, sweet girl that she was, she rolled over onto her back, submitting.

And then they attacked. First the huge one—I saw all at once that he was an intact male—and then his female counterpart.

I tried to pull Purl away to safety, but the big one was on top of her. There. Was. Blood. EVERYWHERE. Purl was crying, her head shaking side to side, searching for me, looking to be saved. It was a cry I still hear in my worst nightmares. She never fought back.

Then the shouting neighbor lady, who turned out to be a hero, was next to me, hitting the big dog in the head with her cell phone, smashing the phone to bits, yelling for me to hit too. I was screaming, hysterical, helpless, out of my mind.

And then, a man screaming to get out of the way. Pulling me away. Cecily, thankfully, was nowhere in sight.

A gunshot.

Now at a distance, I could see the big dog on top, covering Purl. It didn't stop. So much blood.

Another gunshot. And another. The dog was still attacking Purl.

Finally, on what I later learned was the eighth gunshot, the big dog stopped. Slumped. The other dog ran away.

I broke free of whoever was holding me back and ran to Purl, sure she was dead but hoping, hoping. With all the adrenaline running through me, I picked her up, her legs dangling every which way, all the wrong ways. I realized for the first time that a crowd had gathered, and everyone was yelling. Someone shouted, calling me to a pickup truck, motioning for me to put Purl in the bed of a pickup truck full of people. I looked around, saw that the man with the gun was the neighbor who had originally tried to warn us away, and begged him to get in the truck with me.

As we rode, I covered Purl with my body and begged her to hang on.

It was Sunday, and the first vet office we went to was closed. My dad lived nearby and somehow, he showed up (I was later told I had called him, but don't remember that). We moved Purl into the bed of *his* pickup and drove across the river to the emergency vet clinic, me clinging to Purl, and Purl clinging to life.

Brent met us there, and as they took poor broken Purl into the back, he tried to console me. I sobbed out the story to the people at the desk and couldn't understand why they were looking at me so oddly. Then I looked down, and saw that I was covered, head to toe, in blood. I looked like I had just escaped from the movie *Carrie*.

"Cecily?" I asked Brent. And he explained that Cecily had gotten safely to the other side of the gate but had witnessed the whole thing. Then she had run back to our house to tell Brent, and they had returned to the scene, where the dog's owner had shown up, somehow picked up his huge, dead pit bull, and was walking down the street, shouting promises of revenge to whoever had killed his dog.

Miraculously, Purl survived.

My shoe after the Purl incident.

Turns out, we had taken her to the perfect clinic—most likely the only place in Tulsa where she could have been saved. Dr. Zachary Ricker at Oklahoma Veterinary Specialists performed the surgery. Purl had bullet wounds and severe bruising throughout her chest—and that was the doctor's first concern. Second most critical was her left leg, which had been broken by the weight of the big dog. And third was her right leg, which had been shattered by another bullet. But, Dr. Ricker explained, the fragments might be able to be reconstructed, through the use of an "ex fixator"—sort of a Tinker Toy contraption for bones. They didn't know if they could save her. In fact, the odds were against it and it would be a long road. Also, it would cost around $20,000.

We didn't know how we would pay for it.

But how could we *not* try?

To make a very long story shorter, Purl survived. They didn't know if she could ever walk again—but she did. In fact, she went on to run and jump and eat her way through another seven years. She became the mascot of Loops, often appearing in our ads, and visiting the store to lick all of the customers and beg for treats.

Amazingly, Purl didn't hold her attack against anyone, or against life itself. She never became fearful or aggressive. On the contrary, she became that once-in-a-lifetime pet, with the kindest eyes, and wiggliest butt, and best snuggles.

How did we pay for the surgery? Well, people kept asking me to tell the story, and offering to help . . . but I couldn't bring myself to keep re-telling it. So I wrote about it on an Indiegogo page, shared it with the Loops customers—and to my great surprise, they responded by donating enough to cover nearly all of the vet bills.

Knitters. Are. Awesome.

What happened to the huge dogs' owner? We later discovered that this criminal and a bunch of his friends were dealing guns and drugs, all living in a big house that was owned by another criminal, who had fled to California after being indicted in a Ponzi scheme. The house was being watched by D.E.A. agents, who were probably off-duty on that particular Sunday. Soon after this incident, the house was raided, and they found a large store of weapons, a python, and an alligator in the bathtub. To the end, the owner insisted that the dogs were family pets that slept with their kids.

Purl, after the surgery that saved her life and rebuilt her shattered legs.

And despite the fact that the owner, who called himself Diablo, had been charged in the past when his dogs got loose and hurt another dog, these criminals were apparently able to persuade Animal Control not to put the surviving dog down, and got off with only a $150 fine—the minimum for having a dog unneutered and off-leash within the city limits. There was no way to make them help with Purl's vet bills, no real punishment of any kind.

And finally, what happened to Cecily?

She and I each entered PTSD treatment. Neither of us could shake the nightmares, or the recurring pictures and sounds that kept running through our minds.

And Cecily lost seven pounds in a single week.

Despite her protests, I insisted on looking at the scale. What I saw sent shock waves through me. She was 5'5" and weighed 88 pounds.

That week, she was diagnosed with anorexia nervosa, a condition she still struggles with to this day. In fact, she was already anorexic, but neither her doctor (the eating disorder specialist!), nor her cross-country coach, nor her family, nor even Cecily herself had recognized it for what it was. And we have since learned, through years of education and therapy, that often the anorexic patient herself is the last to know.

Purl didn't know it, of course, but in her suffering, she may have actually saved Cecily's life.

Together with Cecily and her doctor, we opted for Family/ Outpatient treatment—a relatively new but promising approach for treating eating disorders. Growing up, Cecily had never really liked being away from home; she'd always begged off from spending the night at friends' houses. We all decided that an inpatient program would not be a great fit for her at that point.

So once again, I dove headfirst into learning all I could about a major, unfamiliar diagnosis. And boy, was I shocked at what I didn't know. I'd always thought of eating disorders as a sort of "vanity" ailment. So when Cecily was diagnosed, it made no sense to me. Cecily was the least vain, most humble, most altruistic person I had ever known. But I learned the truth: As an introverted perfectionist with OCD and anxiety, Cecily had been predisposed to develop this disorder. The cross-country running and PTSD only hastened (and ultimately exposed) the onset.

And let me tell you . . . at least in my personal experience, compared to anorexia, autism had been a walk in the park.

With autism, Sam had been dealt a lousy card, yes, but there was so much more *hope*. New autism therapies, practitioners, books, and even television shows about people with this diagnosis were popping up every day. Schools had Individualized Education Programs (IEPs). There were viral videos of neurotypical kids showing kindness to kids with autism. Everyone was talking about it. Heck, it had become a popular pastime to speculate on which famous people were on the spectrum. Bill Gates? For sure. Dan Aykroyd, Stanley Kubrick, Andy Warhol, Daryl Hannah, Courtney Love . . . the list went on and on.

By contrast, nobody talked about anorexia, except to body-shame famous people who were "too skinny." It was so taboo. I could see it in the faces of the few trusted friends that I chose to confide in. These were people who had known Cecily all of her life, but when they heard the A-word, their voices inevitably dropped to a whisper. You could *feel* the judgment surrounding this diagnosis. It was palpable.

I had to fight not to become defensive or try to prove to them and to myself that I had not somehow caused this. My mind would wander back to what I had read about autism, back when it was first identified as a disorder. At first, the medical community had attributed its root cause to "Refrigerator Mothers"—cold, unfeeling moms who withheld affection from their children, causing them to become autistic. Of course, that had long since been disproven, but I couldn't help seeing these correlations everywhere, and couldn't help feeling that anorexia was a generation behind autism—still shrouded in mystery, fear, and shame; still vastly misunderstood by the general public; and still under-supported by the medical community as a whole.

Practitioners who specialized in eating disorders seemed almost nonexistent, not just in Tulsa, but across the United States. We were told that all of the best therapists and nutritionists worked in the few inpatient programs dotted across the country. It was very common for patients to go to treatment centers several states away from their homes. I remembered a sweet Loops customer from Colorado, who often came to shop and knit when she visited her daughter at the Tulsa inpatient facility. Now that I was experiencing the same struggle, I vividly recalled the strain around this mother's eyes, and the relief she seemed to experience when surrounded by yarn, or knitting quietly on the Loops couch, if only for an afternoon, before returning to her daughter's side.

I asked Cecily's doctor about support groups for survivors of eating disorders, but to my surprise, there were none locally. The reason? "Everyone is afraid of relapsing," he said. "Talking about it can trigger them. So if they are lucky enough to get well, they try to never look back."

Other dark things that nobody tells you about anorexia: the mortality rate hovers around 10 percent, and most of those deaths are due to suicide. Think about it. If you're an alcoholic, some say you can quit cold turkey. It will be very hard, but you can do it. An anorexic can't quit eating. In fact, she has to do the very thing she loathes, the thing that makes her hate herself, six times a day. Three meals. Three snacks. Every day.

When I would sit down with Cecily at each meal and snack, she would be her usual self—kind, funny, joking around. But as soon as she started to eat, I would watch a dark cloud come across her face. Literally, she would turn into a different person before my eyes. She would lash out at me with angry words. Worse, she would lash out at herself.

With the family therapy, plus weekly appointments with her therapist, nutritionist, and psychiatrist, Cecily began to show signs of improvement, but it was agonizingly slow. The next semester, we decided she would stay enrolled at her high school but work from home. This way, she didn't have to deal with the questions and stares from her classmates, and we could make sure she stuck to her meal plan.

Needless to say, Cecily was the first and last thing on my mind every day. It was during this time that I first heard the saying that "A mother is only as happy as her least happy child." So, so true. And when the child you love so deeply is unable to love herself, is suffering and struggling to get from one hour to the next, well, it's pretty darn impossible to think of anything else.

I tried to look at work as a respite from worrying about Cecily, to use the time at the stores or at my computer as a break to focus on something positive and lighthearted. But of course, it became even more difficult to give both Loops stores the attention they needed.

And I was *still* working in the branding business.

As the demands of the two stores grew, and inventory became more difficult to manage, my owner draws became spottier, and there was always some new cash need popping up.

By this point, I was nine years past my initial, self-imposed deadline to exit the branding business. As much I longed to focus my work time entirely on Loops, it seemed that for now, we had no choice but to continue running both businesses.

I will just say it.

I. Was. Exhausted.

No, more than that. I was exhausted with being exhausted.

Money got still tighter—at Loops, and at home. Insurance didn't cover the cost of Cecily's treatment, which was significant. She had separate appointments with a therapist, a nutritionist, and our family appointment with her psychiatrist, every week. All three kids were in private school. Moving Sam or Cecily wasn't an option, and it seemed unfair to move Mallory, who had grown up with her classmates. More and more often, we were holding our breath when the time approached to make the mortgage payment. We tightened up the budget, stopped taking trips, stopped eating out. Took a harder look at the cable bill, the phone bill, made sure to turn out lights when we left the room. We cut costs everywhere we could.

Billie Anne, Loops's first bookkeeper, left Loops to start her own business. So I was, for the first time, managing the day-to-day budgeting for everything: Branders, Loops, and our personal family finances. This forced me to be more realistic about Loops's cashflow, and I had to be honest. It wasn't looking great. Every trend, every graph had begun to show an undeniable downturn. There was no doubt about it: our inability to combine the inventories of both stores had had a significant negative impact on our online store's growth.

What was worse, I had a growing sense of dread each time I walked into one of the stores. Without really knowing why, too often I found myself snapping at my team, demanding to know why this yarn wasn't moving, or why those shelves were so messy, or why this model or that pattern hadn't been finished yet.

My frayed edges were starting to show.

One day, over coffee with Gina H., she suggested the unthinkable: Had I considered closing one of the stores? What if we closed both, and built a new one halfway between the two?

I immediately rejected this idea. Everything about it felt like a failure. I'd have to let go of some of my team. I'd have to let go of a dream. Worst of all, what would people *think*?

In my lowest moments, I thought seriously about shutting it all down. That would be better than closing one of the stores. I could spin it easier: "Oh, this yarn thing has been a fun ride, but our branding business is just growing so fast, we've got to focus on that." I told myself I'd rather close up shop entirely than have Loops die a long, slow, very public death.

But just when I was teetering on the edge of giving up, hope arrived—in a most surprising form.

It came from Jean Brander, my intrepid mother-in-law.

Brent came home one day from visiting his mom with whom he had shared the struggles we were going through as a family—with Cecily, with our other kids, with running two businesses. He said Jean had been quiet for a while, taking it all in. And when she finally spoke, she took Brent by surprise.

"You can't ever let her close that store," she said. "It makes her too happy."

Something in me broke open when Brent shared his mother's words with me.

Suddenly I could see the enormous amount of fear I'd been carrying around. The palpable pressure. The dread. The denial.

I decided to reach out through a realtor to KingsPointe Village, an upscale shopping center located midway between Loops Utica and Loops South. Did they have any space available? Would they be willing to work with me on build-out costs?

I started making notes. What would it take to shut down both stores and move into a new space? What did we need to do to become growth-positive again? What might the design of a new store look like?

Slowly, slowly . . . I began to see a possible path forward.

And then, after I had worked out the details with all of the landlords, and mapped out a plan, I put on my big girl pants and made the announcement to the Troops. "We're going to close down Loops Utica next month, and Loops South the month after that. We're going down to just one store, but it's going to be the best yarn store on the planet. KingsPointe says they can have our new space ready by August," I said with what I hoped came across as confidence.

I braced myself for the team's disappointment, the disapproval, the acknowledgment of my total failure.

Instead, I got something I never expected.

The Troops began to applaud.

CHAPTER 25

DONE IS BETTER THAN PERFECT

We put together a grand, aggressive plan to transition to the new Loops. While the new KingsPointe space was being built out, we would close down and move the whole Utica store into the South store, then close down and move the whole South store (now containing the inventory of both locations) into the new KingsPointe space and open it. We planned to accomplish all of this within the space of 60 days.

I hadn't factored in the reality that construction always takes longer than you plan.

So, when it came time to move everything into Kings-Pointe, the space was still under construction. We had no choice but to move two stores' worth of stuff into a tiny, empty space next door, while we waited for the new store to be completed.

No one but me really believed that 4,000 square feet worth of inventory, furniture, and fixtures would fit into a 1,000-square-foot storage space, but I was committed! That space ended up being the storage version of a clown car. We just kept cramming it in, until the boxes stacked up to the ceiling! And as the new Loops's opening day drew near, we broke out our dollies once again for move number three, and began schlepping everything out of the storage space, into the under-construction space next door.

Meanwhile, inside soon-to-be-Loops KingsPointe, it was a madhouse. Drywallers, painters, electricians, plumbers, everyone was working on top of one another. As each day ticked by, and we trickled past August into September, I could feel early fall—yarn's high-traffic season—slipping away from us.

But rather than wallowing in the fearful feeling of going into the hole, profit-wise, before we even opened, I chose to focus on motivating the construction crew. Each day, I showed up with coffee or bagels, getting to know the men who held our fortune in their rough, work-hardened hands. I chatted them up, praised their progress, and made sure to express my genuine gratitude to them each day.

One vivid memory stands out. There had been a delay with the circular floating ceiling fixture—a signature feature that I really wanted to carry over from the South location—and the construction crew had to fabricate a new one from scratch. I was there all day, working alongside them, as they put the finishing touches on it. And I was there, at 10 P.M. one night, when the triumphant moment came. Seven strong men, dressed all in white and covered in bits of drywall and paint, hoisted the fixture up over their heads, as two more men anchored it to the ceiling. Everyone held their breath as the signal was given, and the men moved out from under the fixture. It held! Everyone cheered and clapped.

This was going to happen. We *would* open as scheduled!

Bright and early the next morning, I met with the lead contractor, eager to finalize the details of our last construction week before our planned grand opening date the next Saturday. But Randy, "The Wizard of Saws," did not have good news.

The construction crew unites to raise the "flying saucer"
at Loops Kingspointe.

He opened his arms wide, indicating the seemingly end-less stacks of fixtures, slatwall, hardware, computers, and hundreds of boxes of yarn we had moved into the space. Everything was piled up, hopelessly jumbled, and covered with thick layers of construction dust.

"Just look around," Randy said. "Everything's still in box-es. There's no way this will all be ready in a week. We've pushed as hard as we can push. I've been doing this a long time, and realistically, you're looking at another month. I'm sorry."

I looked him in the eye.

"Don't worry about my part. I'll be ready by Saturday. The question is, will you be?"

He looked back at me, a smile playing at the corner of his lips. I could tell he knew it was impossible, but he also knew better than to laugh. "I'll tell you what, we won't hold you back. If you can make it happen, so can we."

The challenge was on.

I got right to work, then and there. I hauled boxes and organized them, laying out the store plan. My dolly was burning rubber! I broke out the power tools and assembled store fixtures. I dusted and vacuumed and deep-cleaned. I only stopped for water or to snarf down a lunch that Brent brought by, barely taking the time to speak to him. I finally stopped after midnight and looked up to survey my progress as I set the alarm on my way out. I then allowed myself a moment of satisfaction, a tiny twinkle of celebration.

In a single day, Loops had gone from a construction zone to a store that was about to open.

The next morning, I showed up to see the space busier than ever. The crew had a renewed sense of energy, urgency. Randy walked in and extended his hand to shake mine.

"Amazing," he said. "How did you do it?"

"I told you," I smiled. "This is happening, and it's happening on time."

"I've gotta tell you, I was having trouble motivating the crew," Randy said. "But they all watched you yesterday, busting your butt. They couldn't believe how hard you worked to get all of this done. And they are with you now, sister. They're going to make this happen for you."

Now that the space was inhabitable and organized, with room to work, I could call in the Troops! And the Loops

Troops rallied, big-time. Everyone showed up, armed with brooms, cleaning supplies, and lots of box cutters. Cartons were opened, new yarn was priced and stacked in a frenzy. Computers were set up. Displays were arranged. And Sherri, our crochet queen, was hookin' like crazy to finish our huge window installation—an amorphous, artistic wave of chains, consisting of hundreds of crocheted loops.

Sherri's crochet window installation wows on the opening day of Loops KingsPointe.

You could feel the momentum building to a crescendo.

Very late the night before our scheduled opening, it was down to just Sherri and me, on ladders, hanging those crocheted chains in our floor-to-ceiling front windows. It was after 3 A.M. when we finally tore down the dust-laden brown paper that had covered the windows during the construction months. We high-fived and hugged as we closed up the store, exhausted but jubilant at what we had accomplished together.

Sherri was up all night getting the crocheted loop installation completed!

Just four hours later, Saturday morning. Grand Opening day. I woke before my alarm went off at 7 A.M. I expected to be bleary-eyed. Instead, I felt more rested than I had in years. An enormous wave of peace washed over me. I knew, I *knew*, that I had made the right decision.

Loops KingsPointe officially opens!

This wasn't a failure.
Not at all.
This was a new beginning.

A raised, exposed ceiling and lots of white makes Loops KingsPointe the perfect, modern backdrop for a riot of colorful yarn.

From that Saturday forward, Loops was a whole new company.

And there was something I hadn't anticipated at all.

I knew that going from two stores to one would solve our e-commerce inventory problem. I knew that it would simplify our buying and streamline expenses. I knew that it would be easier for me to be present, to show up and lead from a single location.

But what I didn't expect was the energy.

The energy of having the whole team in one place. And the energy of having all the *customers* in one place. It was palpable. There was no more North vs. South, no "us vs. them." There was only *us*.

It was nothing short of amazing.

And the sales reflected it too. Instantly, sales shot up to surpass the combined total of the previous two stores.

Each day was filled with more joy, more energy, and more laughter in the store than the day before. And things improved at home too. Cecily was doing much better and had returned to school for her senior year. Sam was headed to Oklahoma State University, to study geography (of course!) and had joined a fraternity. Mallory was thriving, playing field hockey, loving school, and even modeling (begrudgingly) for Loops.

Loops KingsPointe, shiny and new.

I didn't know if the Grand Opening lift in Loops sales would last. I didn't know how we would fare through the off-season of spring and summer. But for the moment, I decided to let myself relax just a little and revel in the joy of the new Loops. What I had worried might be perceived as a great failure, my worst humiliation, had turned out to be a great new beginning. There was still so much to do, so much to learn and improve. But for now, the big move was done. And done was better than perfect.

CHAPTER 26

THE BIG SHOW . . . THAT WASN'T

About a year after Loops KingsPointe opened, we decided to try something we've never done before.

For years, customers had been asking us, why doesn't Loops apply to be a vendor at one of the consumer trade shows, like Vogue Knitting LIVE! and STITCHES Events?

At these shows, yarn brands, independent yarn dyers, and some yarn shops create pop-up shops in public venues, like convention centers and big hotels, and offer their wares for sale. It was a significant source of income for a lot of companies, at least in the pre-COVID-19 days.

Fueled by the success of the new Loops location, and perhaps feeling we could do no wrong, we decided to jump in with both feet. We booked a large booth at STITCHES Texas—an inaugural event for the STITCHES organization, to be held in the Dallas area.

In my typical blue-ocean style, I decided our STITCHES booth would be unlike any other, before or since. Instead of crowding it full of displays dripping with yarn, our booth would reflect the Loops aesthetic—airy, clean, and modern, with lots of space to walk around. We lined the walls of the booth with little Binkwaffle yarn bags, each filled with yarn and a pattern, a simple kit. In the middle we placed a chic little sofa and shag rug, so weary shoppers could sit down, chat, and get to know what Loops was all about.

Even though we had lots of experience creating trade show booths for clients through our years of work as branders, Brent and I struggled to get the booth together on time. It was a lot more work than we expected, and we hadn't brought in enough of the Loops Troops to help in the process. By the time we'd loaded everything into a U-Haul and were bouncing down I-35 together, it had dawned on us that really, we had no idea what we were doing. But we were determined to enjoy the adventure—our first time away together since we'd started having kids a decade before.

And we *did* have a lot of fun together that weekend.

What we didn't have was sales.

Or customers.

To begin with, the event as a whole turned out to be an epic flop, with a reported 90 percent less traffic than the typical STITCHES event. Turns out, the DFW Fiber Fest—a much more established Dallas event—had taken place just the week before, so the area's knitters and crocheters were all shopped out.

But beyond that, we learned a really big lesson.

In my haste to swim for the blue ocean, we had neglected to do our homework.

I had never attended a STITCHES event. If I had, I would have known that knitters actually flock to the most cluttered booths—the ones with the most people, the most activity, the most *yarn*.

I would have realized that the best way to stand out, in this case, would have been to pack our booth with our exclusive yarns, Loops original patterns, and kits that STITCHES customers had never seen before.

Worse yet, in making this strategic error, I squandered our best advantage—as a new vendor, we had a special status and recognition in the vendor program. The few shoppers that were there were curious about us and eager to check out the newbies.

But when they got to our booth, they were puzzled. They didn't know how to shop what we had to offer. So they just moved on.

As Brent and I packed up our unsold kits, put our tails between our legs and prepared the drive of shame back to Tulsa, I made note. Next time I took on a big new initiative, I would do my due diligence. I would put in the work. I wouldn't make the arrogant mistake of assuming I knew a better way before I'd checked out the competition and understood what the customer really wanted.

CHAPTER 27

PROTECTING YOUR ENERGY

The weeks after Loops KingsPointe opened were a time of reflection, a time when I looked back and saw lots of dots connecting.

It was then that I realized Sam's autism diagnosis had opened up a deeper well of energy reserves than I'd ever known I had.

And it was then that I thought back to the dark weeks after Mallory was born, when, through a series of unfortunate events, I developed a deeper appreciation for my life, and for the importance of protecting my energy.

In late February 2001, our third child, Mallory, was born.

And six weeks later, I almost died. Twice.

The old wives' tale has it that each successive baby will be bigger than the last. In an effort to avoid having a 15-pound baby that might land me in *Guinness World Records*, I'd determined *not* to gain 60 pounds this time around. I got a personal trainer, watched my diet really carefully, and only gained 35 pounds with Mallory. So I was expecting delivery to be a breeze. Surely she would be a perfectly average-sized baby who would come shooting out on the first push. Right?

Wrong-o.

On the appointed day, I checked in at the hospital for our scheduled inducement, and at first, things were going along swimmingly. Despite the inducement, I was determined to have the most natural birth I could, and to avoid an epidural if at all possible.

But things were moving slowly. The really nice labor nurse kept offering me the epidural, thinking it might "speed things up." And, unbeknownst to me, she had an agenda. That night at midnight, St. John Medical Center was going to turn 75 years old. And the first baby born after midnight would win a big prize package—balloons, diapers, onesies, the works. This nurse and I had bonded, and she was secretly hoping I would be the big winner—and that the winning would happen during her shift. So she was doing everything she could to help things along.

So, at her fourth suggestion, I finally accepted the epidural.

But the nurse's well-intentioned plan backfired.

My contractions slowed down, then came to a halt. For the third time in three pregnancies, they started talking about a possible C-section. But after avoiding a C-section for this long, I was very, very, VERY determined not to have one. So it was decided that I would try pushing first, and if that didn't work, it would be operation time.

I pushed.

And pushed and pushed and pushed and pushed and pushed . . .

For more than two hours I pushed. Mallory didn't appear to be cooperating. Apparently, she was all comfy-cozy in there and not ready to make her entrance.

In a last-ditch effort, they had me turn on my side and push that way.

It was incredibly awkward, and more than a little acrobatic—but it worked! My beautiful baby was born! She was covered in bruises from the birthing process, which led to jaundice in her first week of life. And at her two-week check-up, the pediatrician discovered she'd actually broken her collarbone somewhere along her trip down the birth canal. (No wonder she cried so much those first two weeks!). Don't worry, he assured us, her collarbone would heal quickly on its own. So we "settled in" to adjust to having our third new baby at home.

But, as the days passed, I couldn't shake the feeling that something was wrong. Not with Mallory. With me.

I was tired. So, so tired. I told myself, "Of course you're tired. You've got three kids under five and you're running a business! Give yourself a break."

But life was like moving through wet cement. Getting out of bed, preparing meals, even breastfeeding—everything became a struggle. Each day, each hour, was harder than the last. Was this what it was like to raise three children? Was this what the rest of my life was going to look like?

Brent was exhausted too. He was having to pick up all the slack, and I could feel his resentment building. I thought he was actually angry at me for having a third child, for putting our family in this situation. I just wasn't thinking clearly, starting to feel isolated and even a little hopeless. Our conversations had been reduced to the bare minimum. It was mostly one-word sentences: "Lunch?" "Bath time." "Bedtime."

When Mallory was five weeks old, we decided to take a weekend trip to Kansas City, to shake off the cobwebs and have a little family fun time together. But all I remember is walking around the Kansas City Zoo in a daze. Sam and Cecily would run ahead with excitement, and Mallory was in a carrier on Brent's back, and all I could do was smile weakly as I dragged behind.

Would my energy ever come back? *What was wrong with me?*

The next week, I showed up at my obstetrician's office for my six-week checkup, with Mallory in tow in her baby carrier. No big deal, just the usual formality appointment, I'd thought. I'll just bring Mallory with me and give Brent a little break.

But when my doctor began the exam, things went very wrong, very fast.

First I saw the look of concern cross the doctor's face. Then I heard what sounded like water, hitting the tile floor like someone had turned on a tap.

I was hemorrhaging. I couldn't stop bleeding—a lot—and nobody knew why, or how to stop it.

"Whirrrrrrr" went the sound of the exam table as I watched my legs go up into the air, and my head lowered almost to the ground. From my upside-down position, I could see lots of nurses' legs in scrubs, scurrying around. My cool-cucumber doctor was *yelling*. And as I watched in horror, someone took Mallory's carrier and left the room.

"Doctor, what's happening? I'm kinda freaking out here," I said weakly.

"Shelley, I'm kinda freaking out too," she said.

The next thing I knew, they were sliding me onto a gurney, squeezing the gurney into the elevator, and then taking me across the street—right in the middle of the road, in my hospital gown!—over to the St. John emergency room.

It turned out that my unproductive contractions during labor had likely led to a condition called "retained placenta." The placenta, which normally comes out after the baby, hadn't entirely left my body. Normally they catch this during delivery, and if not, they catch it while the new mom is still in the hospital. But for some reason—perhaps with all the hoopla when Mallory "won" that 75th anniversary award—they hadn't caught it with me. *For six weeks.*

Turns out, this is a pretty precarious situation.

I survived that first hospital hemorrhage, and they sent me home, thinking they had resolved the problem, not expecting further issues.

Wrong-o again.

A few days later, after nursing Mallory, I hemorrhaged again. This time I was at home and collapsed on the bathroom floor. The ambulance came, and off I went to the hospital. It was time for surgery.

I insisted that I bring Mallory, so I could continue to nurse her as much as possible, pre- and post-op, while Brent stayed home with Sam and Cec.

I remember waking up from surgery, and instead of feeling groggy and tired, I felt an unbelievable surge of vitality. I wanted to jump out of the bed and run a marathon! I could feel it in every cell—I WAS BACK.

And in that moment, I recognized the tremendous energy deficit that my poor body had been operating from. It was such a tangible thing, the difference between my "whole" self, and the shell that I had been living in as I dragged from day to day, unknowingly hemorrhaging, barely sustaining, with no joy or zest for life. In my determination to just keep on keeping on, I had ignored the most basic things my body had been trying to tell me. I had been stubborn, I had been stupid, and it had almost killed me.

And I had a big revelation: my energy matters.

I needed to take care of it. Without my energy, I couldn't be here for my kids, for my husband, for myself. I could do lots of things, lots of really hard things, but I couldn't do them all at once. And I couldn't do them alone.

So, many years later, after we had opened Loops Kings-Pointe, I took a pause to step back and reflect. I thought back to my near-death experience. I took stock of my energy, and asked myself a series of questions:

What kind of wife did I want to be?

What kind of mom did I want to be?

What kind of legacy did I want to leave my kids?

Was I fulfilling my true purpose?

Was I making a difference in the world?

If I was going to keep growing Loops, if I was going to make a global impact while sustaining my energy, it was time to work smarter, not harder. It was time to get really clear on the Loops mission, and then build on our culture, with a fully empowered team that would rally around that cause with me.

WHAT TO REMEMBER AS YOU MOVE AHEAD:

Sometimes you have to unravel. Taking that trip to the frog pond isn't something you have to dread. In fact, you can learn to embrace it. The "failure" of our second store . . . the "failure" of our STITCHES booth . . . even the catastrophes like the attack on Purl and the post-natal hemorrhaging . . . each experience presented an opportunity to back up, learn, grow, and potentially create something better.

Lean into your creativity when you pivot. Each time I built a new store, I looked for new ways to bring my creativity to the table. Building the flying saucer ceiling fixture, the button display, the crocheted art installation—each of these projects gave me something positive and creative to focus on, renewing my enthusiasm for the pivot. And while you're in the process of pivoting, never forget: Progress is better than perfect. Not all mistakes require a complete unraveling. Sometimes it's okay to say the mistake is just a design variation and move on.

Look before you leap. The STITCHES event, while an expensive mistake that cost Loops about $20,000, in the long run has saved us millions, because I learned how important it was to study the situation before forming a strategy. Always remember to put your customer empathy hat on before getting carried away by your own creativity. At the same time, when you do make a mistake, recognize that it doesn't always require a complete do-over.

Protect your energy. Recognize when your edges start to fray. Just like a knitter needs to know when she's getting tired, and it's time to put the knitting away before she really messes up . . . the entrepreneur needs to recognize when it's time to take a break, rest, and renew. Build the breaks in wherever you can—little breaks every day, weekends, vacations. Know the work will always be there for you when you get back. But if you're burnt out (or lying in a hospital bed), you can't really serve anybody.

Your Fourth Move

NURTURING THE CREATIVE TEAM

CHAPTER 28

THE FIRST LOOPS TROOPS

As an entrepreneur, I think one of the scariest steps is hiring your first employee. We go into business for ourselves for the freedom, don't we? The joy of absolute autonomy, of being your own boss, of not having to answer to anyone else.

And then, just when everything starts to click along, we realize we need help. If we're going to grow, we can't go it alone. We're going to have to become *someone else's* boss.

It can be really daunting.

But now, looking back, if I could do Loops all over again . . . the one thing I would absolutely do sooner is get more help, earlier and more often.

And I wouldn't just hire more employees. I'd hire more experts. More independent contractors. I'd find more consultants, more mentors, more peer groups. I'd read more books, take more courses, join more memberships. And I'd do all this, not to put off or avoid taking action, but to take more action, sooner.

The day I got that first lease offer for Loops in Utica Square, and I realized that in just a few short months I'd be running a yarn store, a branding business, and a family all at once, one thing was abundantly clear: I couldn't do Loops alone. I was going to need help—lots of help.

I had no clue how to start hiring. I was scared to put an ad in the paper, fearing I might be inundated with applications from knitters. I thought it was surely *every* yarn lover's dream to work in a yarn store! And I knew I didn't have time for a bunch of interviewing. There was far too much to do. (It didn't occur to me at the time that if I hired well, there would be less to do. Chalk it up to panic.)

Instead, I decided to try to hire Emma.

Emma was the sweet German lady who was always knitting in a corner at the Utica Square Starbucks. She knitted faster than anyone I'd ever seen, and her work was beautiful, perfect, exquisite. She had excellent taste in yarn and patterns. She and I often chatted when I ran into her while grabbing my latte, and we'd gotten to be fiber friends.

Just one problem: she worked at the Queen Bee's store.

Apparently she had gone to work at the other store in the years since my last fateful shopping experience there. But she seemed so friendly. Maybe, just maybe, she wasn't loving the toxic atmosphere at the other store. And I saw an opportunity: she was already familiar with the yarn business, which would be a huge help to me.

I decided to broach the subject over coffee.

I told her about my vision for Loops. I even shared my most prized secret idea: The Hot Loops Wall. Emma's eyes widened as I detailed my vision for a more modern yarn store, how I had secured the lease, and how I planned to open Loops Utica in May. Then I invited her to join me.

She wrestled with it for a few days. I think the practical side of her was thinking "a bird in the hand is worth two in the bush." Should she give up her comfortable, safe job at the established store, or take a chance with this young, crazy dreamer?

In the end, crazy dreamer won out. That, and the chance to see and order *all the yarns* she'd always wanted.

So Emma and I got to work. Starting with the marathon buying session with Dave, then other reps, then weeks of pricing carton after carton of yarn on my back porch. She continued the pricing as I turned my focus to the store design, choosing and implementing the point-of-sale system, and hiring the rest of what would become our first group of what we decided to call the "Loops Troops."

My vision for this initial team was, in a word, variety. I wanted a variety of faces, ages, and backgrounds, greeting and assisting the customers who came into Loops. From personal experience, I loved going into local boutiques where you could connect with different salespeople, each with a different perspective and personal aesthetic. I thought that by implementing a rotating schedule of Troops (as opposed to a single manager working the store day after day), everyone might come to work a little fresher and more excited to welcome the customers. Plus, this would give them time to knit on their days off, so they would always be full of enthusiasm for their latest projects, to share with each knitter who walked through the door. More knitting time at home would also mean more knitted samples for the store, which I knew were key to selling yarn.

"Knitters buy projects, not yarn," was some of the best advice Dave the yarn rep gave me.

My second hire for our first Loops store was Gina H., an amazingly creative multi-crafter. She could knit, crochet, spin, quilt, sew—you name it. She was always dressed both colorfully and to the nines. She was up on all the latest designer trends.

Gina didn't so much apply, as simply walk into the job. She told me, in no uncertain terms, that she was coming to work at Loops. End of story. She had a way of graciously refusing to take no for an answer that was compelling. And I knew right away that she was going to be more than an amazing salesperson. She was going to be a good friend.

In hindsight, it's clear that the earliest Loops employees were some of my greatest blessings. I didn't seek them out. They were, I believe with all my heart, *sent* to me. I never advertised, other than hanging a small sign in our front window before we opened. Many of our first team members were customers who were brave enough to ask if we were hiring. Other times, I'd just get a great feeling about somebody's energy, and I'd ask if they were interested in joining us.

There was sunny Annie, the 20-something social worker with the big smile who liked to knit baby blankets; elegant Barbara, who had once been a top manager at Neiman-Marcus in Dallas; quick-witted Kendall, the single mom with the nose piercing who loved making sexy summer tops; brilliant Sherry, who loved teaching and making complex things; practical Billie Anne, our crochet expert and bookkeeper; and good-humored Gene, who loved untangling yarn, helping people fix mistakes, and keeping us all in stitches with his funny stories.

And every Loops Trooper had a unique fiber story to tell. I was endlessly fascinated with how each person had come to take up knitting.

Take Emma, for example. When her father was captured by the Russians during World War II, she was forced to flee her home with her mother and sister. Emma was just five years old. For a time, they sheltered in a bombed-out bowling alley with many other families. To earn money to feed herself and her daughters, Emma's mother knit on assignment for wealthy women. But she could only knit so fast, so she taught her daughters how to knit as well. At the same time, as Emma grew more adept at knitting, she learned to *hate* it. She resented having to spend her days knitting, when she knew that elsewhere, in other parts of the world, other children were running around freely, playing.

The original Loops Troops pose in front of the Utica Square store.

It took decades and many trials and tribulations for Emma to return to her knitting . . . this time, finally, on her own terms. She told me that, now that she was able to choose to knit *what* she wanted, *when* she wanted, she found the process transcendent, even necessary to her well-being. I could see that years of obligatory knitting, under unimaginable circumstances, had helped her tap into a deeper appreciation for the joy of making things on her own terms. It was a gift, something to be deeply treasured.

And, while the other Loops Troopers' fiber stories weren't quite as dramatic as Emma's, we all had this last bit in common: the thrill of making something out of nothing, with just sticks and string. The simple joy of creation.

Although, in those early days, I knew nothing about building a team, about personality tests and leadership styles and employment agreements, I knew this intuitively: the more we could focus on our shared passion, on what we had in common, the more I could make it FUN for them to come to work, the better chance we had of succeeding, together.

CHAPTER 29

STITCHES ARE LIKE PEOPLE

After the initial store opening, as we settled into a sort of ongoing frantic rhythm, I began to dream about getting a top knitting instructor to come to teach at Loops. I knew about knitting celebrities—designers who traveled to teach workshops at local knitting guilds and the larger yarn stores. Some I'd read about in *Vogue Knitting* magazine, others were simply famous names—faceless heroes from my favorite knitting books and patterns.

I knew that a visit from one of these yarn phenoms would bring instant credibility and recognition to Loops. And selfishly, I wanted to learn from them as well. I was willing to invest whatever it took! So I started writing heartfelt e-mails to my favorites, telling them how amazing they were, and asking if they would consider adding us to their next knitting rock star tour.

For a long time, it was crickets. I had flashbacks to trying to get Mr. Helmerich to respond to my business plan.

At long last, I got my first response: politely declining.

And another. And another. They all gave the same basic reason: Tulsa appeared to be too far off the beaten path.

"I'm afraid there aren't any flights that will work."

"This year I'm limiting my visits to a handful of shops near me."

"I might be able to pencil you in for two years from now? Check back with me next year."

Eventually I began to recognize the pattern. The big names (and even the medium-sized and smaller ones) all wanted to go to the same places: the largest stores, guilds, and festivals that were concentrated in the Northeast and the Pacific Northwest.

It didn't seem to matter if I had the biggest, most beautiful yarn store in the world, or if I stocked every pattern they'd ever published, or if I wrote the most appealing invitation, or even if I offered the largest payment.

I wasn't in the Cool Yarn Kids Club.

And because my shop was in Tulsa, Oklahoma ("That's somewhere in the middle, right? Are you close to Texas?"), I'd probably always be an outsider.

I wasn't going to give up, though.

I just adjusted my approach.

I started researching to see which designers were more prone to go farther afield, to venture from the beaten path.

Then I stumbled across a designer named Lucy Neatby. I was initially drawn to her wildly colorful hair, which was dyed the full spectrum of the rainbow: purples, blues, greens, pinks. For me, it was yarny love at first sight. I read a bit more about her: her engineering background, her passion for the complex skill called "double knitting," her lifelong love of sailing, and I sensed the heart of a fellow adventurer. Plus, she lived in a really cool remote location—Big Tancook Island, Nova Scotia—so clearly, she was willing to take the road less traveled.

I dashed off an e-mail to her.

And almost right away . . . I got a YES.

Lucy's visit to Loops was transformative—and not just in the ways I had envisioned. Yes, we sold out every workshop. Yes, it attracted the attention of the stoic Tulsa knitting guild, and even some other regional guilds from neighboring states.

But the biggest transformations were much more personal.

First, Lucy complimented my knitting! I had decided to sit in on one of her classes as a participant. As I sat working my swatch, she came around behind me and commented that my technique was "lovely." It may sound strange, but for someone who MacGyvered her way into this craft, who was knitting alone for so many years, feeling like the odd sheep out, this was the ultimate validation.

Second, I watched the people around me transform. As Lucy explained this very foreign concept of double knitting to my customers, breaking it down piece by piece and peppering her teaching with her unique turns of phrase and funny stories, I watched as one by one, knitter by knitter leaned in. They focused. Their confidence grew before my very eyes. By the end of each class, they were fully converted to the world of double knitting and were chomping at the bit to cast on more projects, to keep learning, keep growing.

It was like those time-lapse videos where a seed sprouts and grows into a plant, then flowers, all in an impossibly small space of time.

And Lucy taught us another lesson, a seemingly simple one. It stirred something deep within me that only recently has truly begun to flower.

She drew a picture like this, to illustrate the anatomy of a stitch:

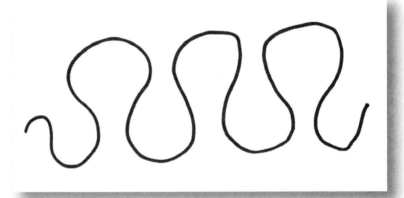

Knitted stitches...

Then she added eyes and smiles, like this:

...they're just like people! Fundamentally connected and happiest in balance.

Lucy explained, "Stitches are just like people." We are all fundamentally connected, one to the next. Have you ever snagged a favorite sweater? If you pull one too tightly, the one next to it gets all scrunched up, and so on down the line. But when a stitch is "happy," it's not pulling too tightly on the one next to it, nor is it too loose. It's just right, content to do its part in holding the whole knitted fabric together.

Lucy's visit unlocked a desire in me to learn from the best, and to share the opportunity with other knitters and crocheters far and wide. And having the de facto endorsement of her visit on our side, suddenly the door to the Cool Yarn Kids Club seemed to open, just a crack.

It was enough for me to attract several amazing instructors to teach at Loops Utica over the following few years: Sally Melville, Louisa Harding, and Gina Wilde of Alchemy Yarns of Transformation. With each visit, I was repeatedly blown away by the depth and breadth of various knitting techniques and styles. And I was fascinated by their fiber stories: how they had first learned to knit, and how and why they left their previous careers to pursue a yarn career full-time.

Each teacher had followed a completely different path, and yet our paths had all converged here, together.

And then there was Helen.

Helen was a knitwear designer that I met at one of the trade shows. A native of Peru, she had authored a book of Peruvian knits, and also produced a line of intricate ready-to-wear garments knit by a group of Peruvian women that she supervised. I was really taken with Helen's approach, and wowed by the garments she had designed. So I was thrilled when she agreed to come teach a workshop at Loops on the weekend of the store's second anniversary. We also planned to partner with a local alpaca farm to have two live alpacas on site, once we got Utica Square to allow us to have an alpaca pen in the middle of the parking lot!

But things started out a bit strange with Helen.

The first little alarm bell went off when she insisted on staying at my home.

Visiting teachers often offered to stay with me, in order to keep costs down. This was apparently a common practice among other store owners, who wanted to ensure that the workshop itself was profitable.

I took a different approach, though. My thinking was that, whether or not the workshop fees covered the hard costs of the event, there were so many other intangible factors that would come from it—ancillary sales in the shop, ongoing sales as knitters expanded their skills, goodwill from the participants who had an amazing experience, goodwill from the teachers who had an amazing experience, and word-of-mouth that would spread to other prospective customers and teachers. In fact, we noticed that the lift in store sales following a single event could last for months!

So I always put our teachers up in the nicest possible hotel, usually an upscale boutique place that was a great representation of Tulsa, like the historic Mayo Hotel.

But Helen was insistent.

"No no no, we will stay together at your home! I always stay at the home of the host," she said.

"Okay, whatever you prefer, but I've got to warn you . . . I have a husband, three small children, and some very energetic dogs."

"No problem, no problem! We will have wine. It will be fine," she assured me.

"All right, if you're sure . . ." (I was already thinking about how I might break this news to Brent.)

"I like *red* wine. *Red*," Helen said.

I made a mental note to stock up.

We moved one of the kids into the other's bedroom, so that Helen could have her own room. I hoped she didn't mind sleeping in a twin bed with a pink gauzy canopy, accompanied by Mallory's substantial collection of stuffed animals.

Once Helen arrived, everything started out fine. I picked her up at the airport and drove her to the store. Her workshop was great; everyone was as taken by her as I had been. She was even more demonstrative than she'd seemed over the phone. As she taught, she often made grand, sweeping gestures and bold, emphatic statements. She reminded me of a Hollywood grandam, a combination of Maggie Smith and Isabella Rossellini.

After the first, very long workshop day was done, we headed to my house. I was exhausted and ready to crash. But Helen had other plans.

"Now we have wine and knit!" she said. I started to beg off, knowing I would have trouble keeping my eyes open for long . . . but again, Helen insisted.

I thought, if I let her outpace me on the wine, and if I worked on something challenging, I would have the best shot at staying awake.

So while Helen did her part, moving rather quickly into a second bottle of red, I pulled out a project that I'd been struggling with for a few months, a dress that I was making with black silk yarn.

There was nothing practical about this project. Every knitter knows that black is the hardest color to work with, because it's so difficult to see what you're doing. And silk is so slippery, you have to work extra hard not to lose your stitches. Add in some intricate lace, and you've got yourself a recipe for yarn torture.

But I had fallen in love with the look of this dress at a trade show, at the Tilli Tomas booth, where they specialized in hand-dyed silk yarns with beads and sequins. Although the owners warned me that they'd never seen the pattern actually made up (other than in the photo supplied by their in-house designer), I had romantic visions of wearing this dress to cocktail parties and business events. It would be the ultimate Little Black Dress for a yarn shop owner.

But my romantic notions quickly dissolved as I tried to work my way through the pattern. It was a mess. None of the abbreviations made sense. The instructions were vague, and I had the strong feeling that they had been written by someone for whom English was not the first language. This was often the case with patterns from German or French yarn companies and I could usually figure it out. But this time, I couldn't put my finger on it; I just knew that much of the pattern had been somehow lost in translation.

Add to that, the challenges of the black, silk yarn and it was no wonder I had privately dubbed this project The Dress From Hell.

As I pulled out my project, Helen asked me what I was working on.

"Oh, I hate to even show you . . . this pattern is a disaster. It's so poorly written, I can't believe I paid money for it. It's obvious the company got the pattern from a designer and just printed it up, without ever testing it or even reading it. It's literally the worst-written pattern I have ever seen."

"Wait a minute," Helen said, squinting in the direction of the pattern. "Let me see that."

I handed it to her.

"I thought so . . .

"That's MY pattern," Helen said.

Ohhhhhhhhhh no. How could this be possible?

And then I realized, there was no designer's name on the pattern. Turns out, Helen had sold them the pattern, and they'd simply branded it as their own design. What were the odds?

In this moment, I thanked the heavens above for the gift of red wine.

I thought Helen would be outraged. But she just seemed highly amused. We had a really big laugh together and, just like that, one of the most embarrassing moments of my life turned into a most fortuitous one, as Helen was able to explain and expand on the pattern. And eventually, I was able to finish the dress! Without Helen's help, I'm convinced that never would have been possible.

THE black silk dress. Complete at last!

While Lucy taught me we are all stitched together, Helen taught me not to take knitting and designing quite so seriously.

And today, now that I count hundreds of designers from all over the world as good friends, I realize that as a collective, they've taught me something much bigger: The value of expert perspectives. As soon as you can, as often as you can, invite in outside perspectives that are different from your own. Resist feeling threatened, worrying that you might somehow look like less of an expert next to them. Invite them in, not for the bump in followers or status it might bring you, but to help light a new path—for yourself and for your customers. The fabric of your brand and your impact will be so much richer for it.

CHAPTER 30

ENTER THE MENTOR

In the middle of the night, a couple of months after the opening of Loops KingsPointe, I couldn't sleep, worrying about the slower spring season that loomed ahead. I grabbed my phone from the bedside table, started scrolling Facebook, and a video caught my attention. It was the Bryan Brothers, the dynamic duo of doubles tennis, teaching doubles strategies.

The videos were good. The information was even better. Right away, I picked up some tips that I knew would help my game. And there was another free video after that, and another. I was fully awake now, actually scribbling down notes at my nightstand, at 2 A.M. The videos were narrated by this guy I'd never heard of, named Will Hamilton. His company was hilariously named Fuzzy Yellow Balls. And it seemed so generous of this Will guy to give away all this valuable content! Then, at the end of the last video, Will made an offer for membership in his Fuzzy Yellow Balls online academy, for a nominal amount.

The whole thing was so brilliant. I'd never seen marketing presented in this way: free content first, then an offer. I searched for the Fuzzy Yellow Balls Contact Us page and shot off an e-mail to Will, right there in the middle of the night. I inquired: How did he come up with this marketing model? How could he afford to give away so much good stuff? And how was it working for him? I was curious—not just as a tennis junkie, but also as a branding professional and as a small business owner.

Did I hear back from Will?

Nope.

So I went back to business as usual at the new Loops and (still!) the branding biz, and I forgot about that e-mail.

But those Bryan Brothers videos stayed in the back of my mind.

Then a few weeks later, I was posting on Facebook for Loops when something caught my eye. Taiu, my friend and owner of Koigu Wool Designs, had liked a page of something called Product Launch Formula, or PLF.

I went to the page, tapped the link, and this guy named Jeff Walker started talking about this method he had developed, where you give away free content, so people can get to know you, see what you're all about, and make an informed decision about your stuff before they buy it.

I knew in my gut: this is what that Will guy had used to market Fuzzy Yellow Balls!

I joined Jeff's list, and soaked up the free videos. It was like he was talking just to me. He talked about "hope marketing"—continually putting out different offers, hoping something will stick. He contrasted that with "launch marketing"—creating a whole event to build excitement, sharing valuable information to help and inspire the customer, whether or not they ultimately chose to buy from you. I loved the excitement this created. I loved the idea of serving my customers in this way. And most of all, I loved Jeff's authenticity and integrity. There was nothing slick about him. He was just a regular guy.

When the offer came to buy Jeff's full course, it was a lot more than I'd bargained for: $2,000. This was right before Christmas, and it would mean some serious belt-tightening for the Brander family. But, because of Fuzzy Yellow Balls, I knew that this method was effective. After all, it had worked on *me*, a jaded marketing pro who had seen everything! I knew I had to try it.

Now, I just assumed that *everyone* who paid $2,000 for an online course would consume all the content as fast as they could, and act on it accordingly. Right? So I committed to watch every module the day it was released, print out every worksheet, and do the work.

Wall full of my notes from Jeff Walker's Product Launch Formula course.

Each week, I couldn't wait for the next PLF module to debut. I set aside a day each week, watched it all, took notes and posted them on my wall, which was rapidly filling up. There was a lot to take in.

And by the second module of PLF, I already had the idea for my first product launch.

I would curate kits with luxury yarn, hand-dyed in colors you couldn't get anywhere else. We'd design an on-trend, effortless pattern to go with each yarn, plus add some fun extras, and ship it all out on the same day each month, to yarn lovers around the country. We'd aim to teach a new skill with each kit and have video tutorials to go along with it.

We would call it LoopsClub.

I'd never had (nor belonged to) any kind of online membership that sent out kits. I had no idea what tech we would use, or how we would build it. But Jeff's program had convinced me . . . done is better than perfect. We would find a way.

We launched LoopsClub in March 2014, just three months after I'd purchased Jeff's program.

In seven days, we sold 500 three-month memberships, for a grand total of $75,000.

Then, much like after I'd gotten that first lease deal from Mr. Helmerich and Utica Square, 10 years earlier . . . now we had to figure out how to make it happen.

It was messy, but we got it up and running. We openly called it a beta launch, so our customers would know we were pretty much making it up as we went along. Turned out, they loved being part of a grand experiment, on the cutting edge of what was happening at the forefront of the yarn world.

And after three months, we knew we had enough know-how to keep it going, so we launched again—this time, offering memberships as a month-to-month option. Sales total for this second LoopsClub launch: $150,000.

All at once, I could see this would solve the seasonality struggle that had plagued Loops for the past decade. No longer would it be "feasting" with big yarn sales in fall and winter, and "famine" as we struggled through the off-season of spring and summer. A membership meant consistent cash flow, month after month.

The predictability of a membership meant that we could buy with confidence, knowing that we would turn around and ship the yarn out as soon as it arrived. Yet another veil of fear and doubt was lifted, as we wouldn't be constantly struggling to turn over inventory and move the slower yarns.

Piles of LoopsClub "blue swag bag" kits, preparing to ship out.

With less fear came more creativity, and I found myself designing the patterns for many of the LoopsClub kits myself. I had no training as a designer, but I knew what I liked to knit: simple, relaxing patterns in luxurious fibers, projects that came off the needles quickly and were easy to style and wear. Often when I chose the yarns for the kits, I'd have a clear idea for a pattern that would make the most of the yarn and be simple and fun to make. It was incredibly rewarding to take my vision all the way from yarn and color development, to design, to styling and photography, to hundreds of blue bags being packed and mailed off. Ready to delight—and unite!—all those fiber friends around the country and, increasingly, around the world.

In our fourth month of LoopsClub, as we were packing up kits in what was becoming a pretty major assembly-line operation, I checked my e-mail and there was a message from Jeff Walker to all of his students. He was announcing a contest. If you've had success with PLF, he said, I'd love for you to make me a quick video about what it's done for you and your business.

I didn't even wait to hear what the prizes were. I was so filled with gratitude for this man, what he had taught me, and how it was transforming my life. I walked out of the back room where the team was packing LoopsClub bags, held my phone up in selfie mode, and hit record. I thanked Jeff from the bottom of my heart, and told him what PLF had done for me, for our team, for our customers, and for our family. Then I hit Send and went back to packing kits, not really hoping for anything, just feeling good to have expressed my thanks.

The next week, I got an e-mail marked "personal"—from Jeff Walker. My heart pounded as I opened it. I had been chosen as a semifinalist in the contest. Jeff's son, Dan, would be coming to Tulsa to film a "case study" with me! I couldn't believe it.

When Dan arrived, I was really nervous, but he put me at ease immediately. He was so young—in his 20s—but had an uncanny ability to quickly absorb my story and create a whole narrative around it. In a single morning, we filmed in three separate locations: at my house with my family, at Loops, and on the tennis court (yes, my weird forehand would now be on display for the whole PLF world to see!).

A week later, when I saw my case study edited and polished, I was overcome with emotion. Dan was one of the most talented visual storytellers I'd ever met in my 25-plus years of branding and production. The tears flowed as I watched myself speak about the fear that I'd been holding on to all of those "North vs. South" years, and the enormous relief that I'd experienced once I allowed myself to risk failure, opened the new store, found PLF, and started LoopsClub. All of a sudden, I could see the 30,000-foot view—where we'd been, and where we were headed.

And then I won the whole case study contest!

And as it turned out, part of my prize package was a free trip to *PLF Live*, Jeff's annual in-person event. That year, it was in Phoenix. I had no idea what to expect. As I walked into the event center and saw a thousand entrepreneurs, jumping up and down to the White Stripes' "Seven Nation Army," my first thought was, *Well . . . this is gonna be different.*

And then Jeff opened with a group meditation/visualization—again, a first for me—and it had a profound effect. I found myself visualizing vividly, flying at 10,000 feet, looking down over the next 10 years of my life. I envisioned myself traveling around the world, connecting isolated knitters and crocheters everywhere, uniting them in their love of fiber and creativity. I didn't know what this meant, or how it was going to happen—but the experience was amazing.

I was so deeply moved by the visualization, I forgot to be nervous about my case study. And before I knew it, there I was on the big screen, with a thousand people hearing about my business struggles and transformation.

At the next break, a bunch of people approached me, wanting to hear more about my experience. I wasn't expecting this, and I was a little embarrassed when I saw a line had actually formed! It was weird, and I'll admit it probably went to my head a little bit. I was seriously floating high on the events of the morning.

By the time a girl I'll call Anna stepped up to talk to me, I wasn't listening very closely. She asked if I had ever heard of a calligraphy summit. I was thinking, *Why are we talking about calligraphy? Is that even still a thing?* But soon she was explaining how she had partnered with some calligraphers who were well known on Instagram, had put together something called an "online summit"—*whatever that was*—and it had turned out to be a pretty big success.

Trying to seem interested, while glancing behind her at the next person in line, I absentmindedly asked, "Oh? How successful?"

And when she answered, she got my attention—100 percent of it.

Then she went on to suggest that we meet and talk about possibly partnering to do a knitting summit. Although it was intriguing, my initial internal reaction was a big fat NO. I was *way* too busy. It would be a huge distraction.

But, much like that long-ago dream to open a modern yarn store, this idea kept whispering in my ear.

I wonder if anyone in knitting has ever done something like this?

What if I could convince some of the top designers to do this with me?

It would be pretty cool to combine my production background with my knitting experience.

Maybe we could try it, just once, and see how it goes.

And every entrepreneur reading this book right now knows what happened next. True entrepreneurs find it virtually impossible to resist the lure of a bona fide game-changing idea, one that has the potential to really change the world.

I took the meeting with Anna.

I found out, years later, that she had actually planned ahead to be in my line that day. She had seen my case study in a launch e-mail that Jeff had sent out, and she guessed that I would be at the live event. She had done her homework, and it was about to pay off. For both of us.

I'm not sure why it took me nearly a full decade of e-commerce experience to find my first online marketing mentor. I only know that I'm incredibly grateful that I started with one of the best. Today, I'm a member of Jeff Walker's Platinum Plus mastermind, so in effect, I now work with a whole host of mentors from every online space imaginable. Jason has helped me and my team dial in our customer experience. Annie has helped me grow as a leader and develop the Loops leadership team. Michael has helped me make our offers clearer and more dynamic, a more accurate reflection of the products themselves. Stu has helped me get clearer on my mission to Knit the World Together, and how to grow the movement. I could go on and on.

(Oh, and it turns out, Will Hamilton is in Plat Plus with me. I still give him grief for never answering that e-mail!)

My point to you is this: Find a mentor. Find *many* mentors, as many as you can, and hire paid mentors as soon as you can afford them. If you can't afford personal coaching, explore the ever-expanding world of online courses and memberships, checking out all the free material first, to find the best fit. Then do the work. Show up. Soak it all in. And when you've started to gain some traction—even when you've grown to the point that you are mentoring others—*get more mentors*. Never, never, never stop learning.

CHAPTER 31

PARTNERS, BREAKING UP, AND BREAKING THROUGH

Shortly after that first *PLF Live*, Anna and I agreed to partner and create the world's first all-online knitting summit.

We found we worked really well together. Anna had studied urban planning in school, had worked for Apple, and was very logical and methodical. It was the perfect balance to my creative, Kolbe 10+ Quick Start strengths.

We agreed that, generally speaking, Anna would handle the tech, financials, and customer service structure, and I would handle the marketing, creative, and production. But we knew, as a startup with no employees, we would both be wearing *lots* of hats.

We started by brainstorming names for the event. Anna suggested Modern Knitting Summit, and I was mulling it over when an idea that I loved finally hit me. I sketched it out and texted the sketch to Anna, who loved it too: Our new product would be called Knit Stars.

My original sketch, the day I came up with the name for Knit Stars.

Next, it was time to reach out to some potential Stars, to ask them to teach in our first season. Right off the bat, I experienced a couple of major failures that almost took the wind out of my sails. The first two potential Stars that I approached via e-mail didn't just turn me down—they ignored my requests entirely.

So I got bold. I sent a second request via FedEx package, and even knitted a little star to go inside one of the letters. *Who can ignore a request that comes with something hand-knitted just for them?* I thought.

Crickets.

All those doubts and insecurities from my early days at Loops Utica came flooding back. I was feeling some serious Imposter Syndrome. What if, even after a decade in the business, the biggest players still didn't acknowledge me? What if they think I'm just some slick marketing hack? What if they think Loops is a joke?

Or . . . what if they're just scared of something so new? Hmmm.

I was lamenting about all this to Anna, who had some really great advice. "It's okay if you don't get the biggest names," she said. "It's our first time. Ask people you will enjoy the experience with. Ask the people you'd like to hang out with at a cocktail party."

One person immediately jumped to mind: Amy Small, owner of Knit Collage. While not primarily a designer, Amy was the person I always most looked forward to seeing at trade shows. She had worked for Free People, the bohemian clothing and lifestyle brand, before starting her own yarn company focused on bulky "art yarns." I loved her warmth, her smile, and her energy. I decided to ask her next.

"YES!" was her immediate response.

This emboldened me enough to approach Stephen West, the designer who had visited Loops in 2012 and whose own Star was not just on the rise but shooting into the stratosphere.

Woohoo, another YES!

And from there, like a bunch of sparkly, shining dominoes, the remaining Stars fell right into place.

In that first Knit Stars lineup, each Star so unique from the next, that I had an idea. I suggested to Anna, what if when we go to film them, we don't just film instructional videos? What if we also filmed a documentary-style lifestyle piece about each Star: What inspires them? What's their design process? What makes them tick?

She agreed. But before production could begin, we needed to launch. We needed some funds for production, and we needed to prove to ourselves that the concept would fly.

With all of the free knitting tutorials online, would people really pay $200 for Knit Stars? And how could we sell it, without having anything to actually *show* people?

Eventually, we landed on showing bits of interviews we did with three of the Stars over Zoom. In each video, the Star would share a tip, and I would talk about how much the best teachers had transformed my knitting life, and how I wanted to share that gift with the world.

Everyone's favorite moment of that first Knit Stars launch was when Stephen West opened the cabinets in his tiny Amsterdam apartment, to reveal his own huge stash of yarn and unfinished works in progress. This little voyeuristic moment was like a salve to the "stash guilt" that knitters universally struggle with.

When we opened cart on what we called the Knit Stars 1.0 early bird launch, Anna and I held our breath.

"PING!" went that first sale. Anna looked at the first purchaser's details and saw she was from *Singapore.* What?!

Up until that point, we had both assumed that all of the participants would come from North America. We could not have been more wrong! Turns out, there were thousands of knitters outside of North America and Europe who followed these famous Stars but never had an opportunity to learn from them. When we closed cart after seven days, the very last person to sign up, right before midnight, was from Dubai.

We had plenty to fund production, and we had more than proven the concept. In fact, it had exceeded our wildest dreams.

When all was said and done, and the main launch was complete, more than 2,000 knitters around the globe had signed on for Knit Stars 1.0!

I wanted the workshops to be mind-blowing . . . so we hired Dan Walker to film and edit them. It was a tremendous amount of work, much more than we'd bargained for, to plan, travel, and film the complete workshops of 10 Stars in the space of just a few months. But once the workshops debuted, the response was truly humbling.

The Knit Stars participants positively gushed about their experience. "This has changed my knitting life!" many exclaimed. One person remarked, "I believe you've created the new paradigm for knitting education." Many remarked on the positivity and encouragement of the community we'd built.

And everyone was asking, "Where can I sign up for Knit Stars 2.0?"

Anna and I rolled so quickly into planning for Knit Stars 2.0, we didn't even stop to breathe and consider adding more team members. The next year *more than doubled* the signups of the previous year. And still, it was just the two of us doing all the work, supported by Dan's filming and editing.

For Knit Stars 2.0, we decided that Dan and I would travel to Europe, to film on-site with three of our international Stars—Beata Jezek of Hedgehog Fibres in Cork, Ireland; Nancy Marchant in Amsterdam; and Aimée from La Bien Aimée in Paris. While there, I could film our pre-launch videos using my iPhone.

There was just one problem: I hadn't flown overseas in more than 20 years. And in that time, I had become terrified to fly over the ocean. But I still longed to see more of the world. And I kept recalling that visualization from *PLF Live*, where I saw myself traveling all around the globe.

Knitting at Machu Picchu during filming for Knit Stars Season 4.

During filming for Knit Stars Season 4, the only way to get our luggage and gear to Big Tancook Island was via crane and ferry!

Hanging out with Arne and Carlos at their home in the mountains of Norway, during filming for Knit Stars Season 3.

Then I had an idea. I knew one person so bold and adventurous, she might have enough courage for both of us: my daughter Mallory. This would be a memory we could create together. And it would be handy to have another pair of hands, schlepping camera equipment!

Now, I'm not gonna lie. That first trans-Atlantic flight, from Atlanta to Amsterdam, was daunting. I tried to knit but kept messing up and had to tink back. (For the non-knitters: "tink" is "knit" spelled backward, and it's what we call unknitting your work, one stitch at a time, to fix a mistake.)

Honestly, I think it was the combination of Xanax and champagne that got me through that flight (don't try this at home!). But once we arrived . . . it was pure magic. I had been to Europe only once, in my early 20s, and all of the memories came flooding back. The transformative experience of immersing yourself in another culture. The connections made outside your usual circle that widened your perspective. And most of all, the commonalities that unite us all as humans—the little kindnesses, the smiles, the children running and playing, the adults hugging in airports.

I was hooked.

The trip was a whirlwind (three countries in six days!), but a great success. Nancy, Beata, and Aimée each had fascinating stories. Mallory and I found that we loved working together.

And on our flight back, it hit me. We could take our Knit Stars owners on a new, virtual journey each year. Visit different areas of the world. Shed new light on traditional knitting and crochet techniques from all corners of the globe. Broaden perspectives. Open minds and hearts. Connect more and more yarn lovers in an ever-widening circle of positivity and creativity.

We had big dreams.

We were going to need more help.

Heading into Knit Stars season 3, Anna and I hired our first employee, a project manager. And almost right after that came a couple of major developments: The project manager announced she was pregnant. And Anna offered to let me buy her out.

Even though we had just completed our biggest launch by far (more people had signed up in the Knit Stars 3.0 early bird launch than for all of Knit Stars 2.0 combined!), Anna's desire to exit the business didn't come as a complete shock. She had recently undergone a major life transition and was yearning to simplify and focus on her calligraphy business and related products.

Also, she and I had begun to find ourselves on opposite sides of various issues. I was always looking to improve and optimize Knit Stars, adding more features and up-leveling the production. Anna was always looking to automate and put things more on autopilot. And having an employee definitely complicated things. In some ways it felt like we had gotten married and had a child—and that the early "romance" had gone out of the business relationship.

And so it was predestined that the most fulfilling year of my life thus far was also the most stressful.

I was literally living my dream, reveling in working my purpose through Knit Stars and Loops. But at the same time, dissolving the partnership with Anna was like going through a long, drawn-out divorce while still living in the same house as your partner.

The height of the discomfort came when Anna insisted on accompanying me, Mallory, and the cinematographer on our Knit Stars 3.0 production trip. We were headed to Finland, Norway, and Denmark, and Anna had always wanted to visit Norway, where she had traced part of her ancestry. The trip was like a microcosm of the year—invigorating, creatively fulfilling, life-altering . . . and unbelievably awkward, all at once.

As the saying goes, it was the best of times, and it was the worst of times.

Worst: the airline lost my luggage, and Mallory's, on the flight into Amsterdam, and we didn't recover it until seven days (and three countries) later.

Best: I learned how far you can go on one sports bra, a pair of leggings, and a T-shirt. And I've since learned to live out of a carry-on, no matter how long the trip.

Worst: staying at a run-down Norwegian hotel without air-conditioning in the country's worst heat wave on record.

Best: swimming in the crystal-clear glacial lake next to the amazing home and garden belonging to Knit Stars Arne & Carlos, then sitting in the sun on their deck, and drinking great wine from a box with their pictures on it.

Worst: trying to film on the beach of Fanø Island, Denmark in 30 mph winds, with Anna holding the camera, and all of us just wanting to wrap for the day and go to bed.

Best: when a naked man emerged from the sea behind Anna and Mallory in the middle of my take, and we all collapsed in a fit of giggles.

Despite the extreme awkwardness of the trip with Anna in the midst of dissolving our partnership, I felt a huge sense of accomplishment when it was done. Now we could both turn our attention to completing the rest of the Knit Stars 3.0 workshops, delivering our best event yet, and winding up our buyout agreement.

But what I hadn't counted on was the "short-timer syndrome" that would naturally set in for the partner who planned to exit the business. Many of the responsibilities—customer service, systems, and tech—began to shift my way, as Anna became less and less engaged and available. At the same time, our negotiations became more difficult, as she hired a hard-driving East Coast attorney who seemed bent on winning at all costs.

It didn't help that I just wanted it all to be done. One of my friends and mentors remarked at the time, "You're too nice. It's like you're playing checkers, and she's playing chess."

When the negotiations became even more difficult, my attorneys, as well as many of my friends and advisors with more experience in such things, suggested that I simply walk away and start over. Why pay Anna anything at all? I had the contacts, the customers, the know-how. Why not just close Knit Stars and start up "Loops Stars"? they asked.

But I had two big reasons: One, I didn't want to lose momentum. Thousands of fiber friends around the world had already placed their trust in Knit Stars. Two—and most important—was an integrity issue for me. Yes, I was probably going to overpay. Yes, I could walk away without paying anything. But if Anna hadn't approached me three years earlier at *PLF Live*, where would I be now? Maybe I would've created a summit on my own. Maybe I would've created something even bigger.

But once the universe had given me this gift, how could I look that gift horse in the mouth?

I thought back, once again, to that empathy lesson from my father so many years ago. And I remembered Melinda's advice that I kept in mind when meeting with vendors: Is this a good deal, *for both of us*?

And so, on December 28, 2018, after almost a year of awkwardness and attorneys, Anna and I finally signed our agreement and she exited the business. She's now moved on and focused on growing her own businesses. We still stay in touch occasionally.

And today, Knit Stars is wholly owned by Loops, run 100 percent by yarn lovers. With a family of more than 50 Knit Stars, and more than 10,000 Knit Stars owners across the globe, united in their love of fiber and their shared goal of Knitting the World Together. Taking full ownership of Knit Stars has allowed me to stretch my skills, build a more comprehensive team, and integrate the Knit Stars offerings with Loops offerings to better support our customers.

What I initially perceived as a break*up* ultimately became a break*through*.

WHAT TO REMEMBER AS YOU MOVE AHEAD:

Expand your team, early and often. Identify your zone of genius—the thing you're the very best at, that lights you up. For me, this is being creative—writing, sketching, designing. Then identify the things that are the furthest from that zone—for me this is tech, project management, and accounting. Resolve to hire people to do these things as soon as you possibly can. If I had listened to my own advice and hired more tech experts from the start, I wouldn't have ended up with a cobbled-together "Frankensystem" that took years to untangle and rebuild.

Widen the circle. Look for opportunities to collaborate—with contractors, experts, peers, and mentors. Look for people with values that align with yours but perspectives and skill sets that differ. And if you buy their courses or memberships, for Heaven's sake, resolve to show up and do the work. Anything less is cheating yourself.

Stay open to partnerships. At first, this might feel like an affront to your entrepreneurial spirit. After all, you got into this to control your own destiny, right? But partnerships don't have to be forever, and they don't have to be 50/50. The right collaboration, right now, could massively multiply your business and your impact for years to come.

CONCLUSION

Moving Forward

When I first set out to write this book, I thought it would be a memoir. People were always asking me to share my crazy story. What possessed me to leave the ad biz and open a local yarn store? How did it grow from a franchise idea, into an e-commerce business, and from there into a global movement to Knit the World Together?

So often, they would end up shaking their heads and say something like, "I don't know how you find the energy. You must never sleep."

That response always worried me. Because in that moment they seemed to be thinking, "*You* did this. Because you have some kind of exceptional energy/skill set/luck. But *me*? I could never do this."

And that's why I decided this book needed to become more than a memoir.

It needed to become a call to action.

Not a prescription, exactly—formulas aren't really my style. But a collection of stories *that shows you what's possible.* A narrative framework that holds the creative space for you to apply the stories to your own life, your own goals and dreams and purpose.

And these are the lessons I most hope you will take with you as you move forward:

YOU WON'T BE ABLE TO CONNECT THE DOTS UNTIL LATER—MUCH LATER.

You don't need all the answers right now. Yes, do your research. Yes, find a mentor (or ten) if you can. But let go of perfection. As Salvador Dalí said, "Have no fear of perfection—you'll never reach it." Just get going.

I think of it like the process of making a sweater. You're knitting along, stitch after stitch and row after row. You keep moving ahead on faith that you'll eventually have something that resembles the pretty modeled photos on the pattern.

Thousands of stitches later, you wind up with a series of flat pieces—a front, a back, two sleeves. Slowly, meticulously, you attach each of the pieces. Then you soak it in water, pin it out. And finally it dries, and you put it on, and hope it fits. If it doesn't, well . . . you gift it to a friend and start another sweater. But now you know more about sweaters. And nothing can take that away.

You keep moving forward, trusting the process, believing in your creativity and knowing the next sweater will fit better than the last.

Now I look back at that girl on that tricycle and realize that all those times I set out on my own, I was practicing what it felt like to forge my own path. Learning to zig when others zag.

Now I know that what felt like, at the time, one of the deepest blows a parent could possibly face—Sam's autism diagnosis—actually opened up a new well of fierce determination and energy that would continue to serve me in every other endeavor the rest of my life.

So don't try to predict all the possible outcomes. Just take the next step. Stitch the next stitch. And don't forget to document the journey—in notes, in photos, in a journal, whatever works for you—so you can keep looking back and seeing how far you have come.

EMPATHY AND INTEGRITY IN ALL THINGS.

That simple empathy lesson that my father gave me so many years ago has become my compass, my true north.

It has served me in all aspects of my life, from creating ads, to partnering with yarn vendors, to working with team members, to grappling with the most difficult issues of our time, including racism. Time and time again, I've seen the power of that seemingly simple act of pausing, listening, and doing your very best to put yourself in the other person's shoes, to *really* work to understand different perspectives before sharing your own.

This is the step that has made the single biggest difference for me, both in business and in life. It's helped me stay rooted in integrity and see the true value of sharing over selling.

If you will keep coming back to empathy, over and over, in every interaction and negotiation and decision, it will become second nature for you too. People will be naturally drawn to you. They will *want* to work with you, to be a part of what you're building.

And the best part is, no matter how little or how much money you may make, you will still know in your heart that you've succeeded.

DON'T BE AFRAID TO FROG BACK.

Experienced knitters understand that frogging—having to "rip it rip it" out and start again—is part of the process.

But beginning knitters almost always resist this idea. In fact, they'll do almost anything to avoid it: Tie a bunch of knots, leave a gaping hole, abandon the project altogether. I've seen many a new knitter dissolve into tears over the idea of going "backward."

As they progress, they learn that what they first perceived as going backward is actually a form of moving forward. They develop a better understanding of the anatomy of their stitches, which helps them learn new stitch patterns. They become empowered, able to proceed without fear, knowing they can handle whatever the project throws at them.

It's the same with your business.

The sooner you can learn to accept "failure" as a natural part of your business, and develop the willingness to learn from those failures, the faster you will grow.

PROTECT YOUR ENERGY.

You hear it all the time: "It's a marathon, not a sprint."

I can't think of any area of my life where this has been more applicable than my entrepreneurial journey.

Especially if you're a creative (and if you're a human, you ARE a creative), your energy is your most precious asset. You must treat it as such. If your creativity bank account goes to zero, it can be very, very hard to muster the energy to fill it back up.

Build balance into your entrepreneurial life. For me, this looks like using a daily planner that's set up to help me give equal weight to my personal and business goals. So when I'm listing out all my business tasks for the week, I also make time to list some personal tasks. Things like "tennis drill," "coffee with Mallory," "meditate every morning," and "remember to knit at least one row every day."

My planner also helps me stay focused on my own zone of genius—because I've realized that any day that starts with writing or being creative, usually turns out, on balance, to be a good day. So every morning from 8 A.M. to 11 A.M. is blocked out for a writing appointment with myself.

My friend Michelle Falzon teaches people to "create without burnout." She says there are five phases to a healthy, sustainable creation process:

1. **Saturate** (where you're researching and learning and absorbing information and experience)

2. **Percolate** (where you give the ideas time to marinate, making new connections and developing your ideas)

3. **Create** (where you do the work and make the thing)

4. **Celebrate** (where you celebrate and acknowledge your creation, yourself, and those who helped you along the way—whether you considered it a "win" or not.)

5. **Rejuvenate** (where you take a minute or a day or a week to rest, restore, and reset—refilling your tank, so you are prepared to begin the process of creating again, feeling strong and ready for your next creation).

And Michelle's point is that all five of these phases are necessary to maintain optimal, sustained creation (and avoid burnout).

Because what happens for most entrepreneurs is they tend to focus on just *two* of these phases—Saturate and Create. Take the brief, then do the job. Do the research, then create the thing. Then rinse and repeat. It's just saturate, create, saturate, create, saturate, create . . . ad nauseum. Until we burn out.

But by adding in those other important steps—Percolate, Celebrate, Rejuvenate—and valuing them as an important part of your creative process, you will not only get a better creation, but you'll also have the long-term stamina, joy, and desire to excel at the marathon that is the entrepreneurial journey.

Don't wait to multiply your impact.

It can be scary to take the next step—most especially, those steps that involve other people. To add new team members. To hire consultants. To form new partnerships.

But do it—sooner rather than later.

You may not know what you don't know. But *they* might.

If I were to do it all again, my single biggest "do differently" would be to get much more help much earlier in the process.

I would have taken careful stock of my strengths and weaknesses and sought out support accordingly—in accounting, in tech, in project management, in hiring and management and leadership.

And then I would have clarified my mission to Knit the World Together and shared it with all of them—every team member, every consultant, every mentor and vendor-partner—every day, over and over.

Now you have the benefit of my experiences. You also have the benefit of the internet and technology that's advancing at truly warp speed, making it easier than ever to "go global," even right from the start.

You're armed with everything you need: Your empathy, your energy, and your creativity.

The world is smaller than you think, and it's out there waiting for you.

So jump on that tricycle and go get 'em.

I'll be right here, cheering you on.

xoxo

Shelley

RESOURCES

I've put together a complete list of resources that have helped me along the way, including:

• The technology solutions I've found most useful in my journey

• The best way to learn from the mentors I've mentioned in this book

• Links to specific strategies and marketing tools I love, and

• A listing of my favorite books and tools I can't live without

I'm hoping you'll find all of this helpful!

Because this list is constantly evolving, I've put everything at one link that we will update on a regular basis. Find it all at: TheNeedleBook.com

INDEX

Page numbers in *italics* refer to photographs.

ACKNOWLEDGMENTS

Thank you to Brent, my partner in life and biggest champion, for always reminding me that the squeaky wheel gets the grease—even on a tricycle. Thank you to the late Jean Brander for telling Brent he could never let me give up on that yarn store. Thank you to Sam for teaching me to trust my own map, to Cec for teaching me how compassion, grace, and tenacity can coexist, and to Mallory for showing me how to just get on the damn plane and fly.

Thank you to Mom and Dad for not giving me back to the hospital when Sherry Blue asked you to, and for instead sending me to Montessori School, where I learned to love to learn.

Thank you to every single Loops Troop team member over the years who helped pick up dropped stitches, reset passwords, kept your cool through all the launches and pivots, and put up with all my crazy-ass ideas.

Thank you to Melody and Patty and Mary and Reid and all of the other amazing folks at Hay House, and for my intrepid early draft readers: Teresa, Karen, Kurt, Michael, Amy, Brent, Mallory, and Dad.

And thank you to all the Loops and Knit Stars fans worldwide who are helping to Knit the World Together. One stitch at a time.

ABOUT THE AUTHOR

Shelley Brander is CEO of Loops Productions, which includes Loops yarn store, LoopsLove.com, LoopsClub.com, and KnitStars.com. She lives in Tulsa, Oklahoma, with her husband Brent, a graphic designer turned full-time painter. Together they have three creative, compassionate grown children, and usually at least three dogs. Shelley is on a mission to Knit the World Together™ and to encourage creatives to put their passion first.

For a complete list of resources to help you pursue your wildest entrepreneurial dreams, visit TheNeedleBook.com.

Hay House Titles of Related Interest

All of the above are available at your local bookstore,
or may be ordered by contacting Hay House (see next page).

We hope you enjoyed this Hay House book. If you'd like to receive our online catalog featuring additional information on Hay House books and products, or if you'd like to find out more about the Hay Foundation, please contact:

Hay House, Inc., P.O. Box 5100, Carlsbad, CA 92018-5100
(760) 431-7695 or (800) 654-5126
(760) 431-6948 (fax) or (800) 650-5115 (fax)
www.hayhouse.com® • www.hayfoundation.org

Published in Australia by: Hay House Australia Pty. Ltd.,
18/36 Ralph St., Alexandria NSW 2015
Phone: 612-9669-4299 • *Fax:* 612-9669-4144
www.hayhouse.com.au

Published in the United Kingdom by: Hay House UK, Ltd.,
The Sixth Floor, Watson House, 54 Baker Street, London W1U 7BU
Phone: +44 (0)20 3927 7290 • *Fax:* +44 (0)20 3927 7291
www.hayhouse.co.uk

Published in India by: Hay House Publishers India,
Muskaan Complex, Plot No. 3, B-2, Vasant Kunj, New Delhi 110 070
Phone: 91-11-4176-1620 • *Fax:* 91-11-4176-1630
www.hayhouse.co.in

Access New Knowledge.
Anytime. Anywhere.

Learn and evolve at your own pace
with the world's leading experts.

www.hayhouseU.com

FREE WEEKLY BUSINESS INSIGHTS
from a MASTER IN THE FIELD

Over the past 30+ years, Reid Tracy, President and CEO of Hay House, Inc., has developed an independent upstart company with a single book into the world leader of transformational publishing with thousands of titles in print and products ranging from books to audio programs to online courses and more.

◆ Reid has dedicated himself to **helping authors create successful businesses around their books and vice versa**, and now he's here to help you achieve success by guiding you to examine and grow the business best suited to you.

◆ The Hay House Business newsletter isn't just about book publishing or becoming an author. It is about **creating and succeeding with your business and brand**.

◆ Whether you are already established or are just getting your business off the ground, the **practical tips delivered to your inbox every week** are invaluable and insightful.

*Sign up for the **Hay House Business newsletter**, and you'll be the first to know which authors are sharing their wisdom and market-tested experience with self-starters and small business owners like yourself!*

Sign Up Now!
Visit www.hayhouse.com/newsletters/business to sign up for the Hay House Business newsletter.